Lincolnshire
COUNTY COUNCIL

COMMUNITIES, CULTURAL SERVICES

Signalman Jones

Tim Parker

Based on the recollections of
Geoffrey Holder-Jones

SEAFARER BOOKS

SHERIDAN HOUSE

First published in the UK by
Seafarer Books
102 Redwald Road
Rendlesham
Woodbridge
Suffolk IP12 2TE
www.seafarerbooks.com

And in the USA by
Sheridan House Inc.
145 Palisade Street
Dobbs Ferry
NY 10522
www.sheridanhouse.com

UK ISBN   978-1-906266-21-9
USA ISBN 978-1-57409-309-4

A catalogue record for this book is available from the British Library

A catalogue record for this book is available from the Library of Congress

Edited by Hugh Brazier
Typesetting by Julie Rainford
Cover design by Louis Mackay

Printed in Finland by Bookwell Oy

Contents

Foreword

Geoffrey Holder-Jones is undoubtedly a very special man, whose tales are told vividly within this book. His stories are presented to us with great modesty, and concentrate largely on his career in the Royal Navy Volunteer Reserve and his service in the Second World War. Yet he is one of many such men who stepped forward at a critical time in the nation's history to boost the naval personnel in order to man a rapidly expanding fleet. Their contribution to the eventual success of our forces has gone largely unreported, and their brave exploits – particularly in the little ships – have been dwarfed by the more famous battles and campaigns which were dominated by the capital ships.

Entry into the RNVR in the Great Depression gave Geoffrey a new lease of life and adventure. It introduced him to mess life and comradeship with its very special naval humour. His stories throughout the book never lose sight of these assets, which form the very basis of life at sea, emphasised still further during the war that was to follow. Danger and violence hit him early, and his Distinguished Service Medal speaks volumes for his bravery, which is casually brushed aside in the narrative. Destined for greater things, he gained a commission – and a wife – and had a gruelling war, largely in converted armed trawlers used for escort duties. His experiences in the storms and ice of northern waters will strike a chord with those who have been there, and can only be imagined by those who have not, and his exploits from the North Cape to the eastern seaboard of America provide for many gripping tales. He was talented enough to gain command quickly and then was captain of six ships, albeit four of them over a period of ten weeks when he was a 'spare' commanding officer for the Western Approach trawlers. This must surely be a record!

After being demobilised at the end of 1945 he trained in Bognor Regis as a teacher and taught in schools around Brighton, with his final job as Headmaster of St Andrew's Church School, Hove. I guess that is where my link with his story starts, for my father left the RNVR as a padre at the end of the war and was Vicar of Bognor before becoming Vicar of Hove and a Governor of St Andrew's School, which I then attended. Yes, I was one of Geoffrey's boys! Later, as a cadet from Brighton, Hove Sussex Grammar School, I sailed in HMS *Curzon* on trips to France, so I can fully vouchsafe his description of how she rolled like a pig.

Finally, I found myself as the guest speaker at Lancing College in 2008 at the dinner where the author Tim Parker first met Geoffrey. I am so very pleased that that evening has led to this book, for the stories told by Geoffrey give a real feel for the fighting Royal Navy in the middle of the last century, and especially the fortitude of the men and women of this country. We owe them a great debt, and we should all be grateful to Tim Parker for putting this book together so ably.

Rear Admiral John Lippiett, CB, MBE

Preface

It was in June 2008 that I first met Signalman Jones. By then he was Lieutenant-Commander Geoffrey Holder-Jones, DSM, VRD, RNVR. We were guests at a dinner at Lancing College in Sussex to commemorate the time when the college had been taken over by the Royal Navy and renamed HMS *King Alfred*. I was seated opposite Geoffrey, who proved to be an excellent dinner companion. A lively and engaging man, Geoffrey told me of his time at *King Alfred*, where he and some twenty thousand other cadets had been trained to become officers desperately needed for the war against Germany. There was just one problem: there was a wide refectory table between us, it was a noisy evening and both of us are a little deaf. Happily, Gladys, Geoffrey's charming wife, was sitting next to me and she filled in the pieces that we missed. I was intrigued, and we arranged to meet. It was then that Geoffrey entrusted his scrapbook to me. As soon as I saw the scrapbook I knew his story was worth the telling.

I have been very fortunate in the number of family and friends who have helped me to become a writer. As a consequence of their help, in all kind of ways, here is my first book.

To begin: Beth has given me love and comfort in my struggles (and corrected my spelling), and Donna with her skills and patience has been crucial in this enterprise.

Then, in no particular order but starting with two visionaries who took a gamble and gave me my first writing jobs: Simon Bradshaw, editor of the *Argus*, and Leonard Stall. Thanks also are due to Neville Dutton for his splendid paintings, and to Hugh Burnett, Roger Clifton-Moore, Andrea and Jim Darch, Patricia Eve and her team at Seafarer Books, Alan Godwin, Simon Hatchwell, Peter James, Andrew Konecki, John Martin, Peter Mulleneux, Robin Norris, Julian Parker, Michael Parrish, the late Peter Rawlings, John Riley, Ian Steel, David Watson, Robert Weir, and others too many to mention.

I am grateful to the Michael and Honor Thwaites Heritage

Association for granting me permission to reproduce two poems by Michael Thwaites, to the Society of Authors for permission to include an extract from one of John Masefield's poems, and to Duggie and Jeannie Wakefield for graciously allowing me to reproduce a letter from Gracie Fields.

Finally, I am indebted to the two people who are most important in all of this, my good friends Geoffrey Holder-Jones and his wife Gladys, with whom I have enjoyed tea and biscuits at 1600 hours on many occasions.

Tim Parker
October 2010

A message from Signalman Jones

I am so pleased that Tim's book is to be published. I told Tim my stories (he tells me that he still has a box full of anecdotes), and he did a great deal of research to check the facts and the background before writing the book. Indeed, he was able to tell me things that I had not known about the great Battle of the Atlantic.

Those afternoons brought back many memories. They renewed my appreciation of the friends I made, and the extraordinary courage of the ordinary men and women who were little mentioned during the war. These individuals did their best for little glory: fishermen on minesweepers, Asdic operators, gunners, cooks, engineers. Seamen from the Hebrides, Grimsby and other fishing ports. Volunteers from Canada, Australia, India, New Zealand, Argentina and others from all round the world, who helped defeat our enemies in what was the British Empire's last sea battle.

And how can I forget New York? America could, with all its might, have survived the onslaught of the German U-boats – but I believe our squadron of twenty-four assorted fishing vessels won the battle for the USA in the spring and summer of 1942.

I must mention four particular friends I made while I was at sea. First, Michael Thwaites, first lieutenant of *Wastwater*. He was a great friend and we spent many hours together. A poet of distinction, an author and a Rhodes scholar, Michael encouraged me to give my own writing a try. Then Archie Hodge, my first lieutenant in *Baffin*. I owe him a lot, and it was much to my delight that he took over my command when I returned to the UK. Then there was Lieutenant Derek Hitchman, later a distinguished teacher in Hove County Boys' School. Derek was an inventor, a scientist, a mathematician and an organist. And there was another great friend, Stuart Thornton, our steward on *Baffin*. I have never known a kinder man.

Of course only a fraction of my life has been lived at sea, and I have so enjoyed the years since the war, with Gladys and my children, and my time as a teacher and headmaster. And I'm so pleased to learn that among my boys was young Lippiett, and that he should become an admiral. This book is a testament to all those who have shared my life, and I remember them with great affection.

Finally, and most important, my sincere thanks to Tim Parker, who did not realise what he was taking on when he approached this ancient mariner, who when asked a question found it nigh impossible to keep to the point. Thank you, Tim, for your good-hearted patience and humour.

Lieutenant-Commander Geoffrey Holder-Jones, DSM, VRD, RNVR
October 2010

1

Early years –
Liverpool and the Great Depression

I had better begin at the beginning and that's a hell of a time ago. I was born in Liverpool in 1915, the youngest son of a draper, Arthur Holder-Jones. It was the second year of the First World War. George V was King of England and his cousin Kaiser of Germany. Asquith was Prime Minister and Winston Churchill was First Lord of the Admiralty.

At the start of the war there had been cheers, brass bands and church bells. There was great enthusiasm and queues at recruiting offices to fight for King, Country and Empire. 'It will all be over in the year – better join up now so as not to miss the fun.' There were some sane voices: 'The lamps are going out all over Europe. We shall not see them lit again in our time,' remarked Edward Grey the Foreign Secretary. And of course he was right; it was a ruinous war, causing distress and hardship throughout the world. And while we won the war the great days of the Empire were over.

Of course I was far too young to have any knowledge of what was happening in Liverpool, never mind the world, and indeed my first memories are not of Liverpool. Before I was old enough to take notice of my surroundings our family, my father, my mother, Alice, my three older brothers, Robert, Raymond and Roland, and I had moved from Liverpool to North Wales. I don't know whether the move was prompted by the great flu epidemic; if it was, it was well done, as none of our family contracted that killer disease. Now it's almost forgotten, but in 1918 at the end of the First World War the country, and indeed the world, was struck by a virulent virus which became known as the Spanish flu. The influenza pandemic was more lethal than the fighting in the war that cut down so many young men. Glasgow was the first city to be affected, and within three months almost a quarter of a million people in the UK had died. So severe was the epidemic that it seemed that the old cry last heard during the Black Death might return to our cities – 'Bring out your dead.' A popular rhyme went the rounds:

I had a little bird
Its name was Enza
I opened the window
And in flu Enza

Liverpool was one of the worst-hit cities, and thousands perished. Liverpool's slum dwellings, poverty and lack of food contributed to the spread of the disease, but it was no ordinary flu. A fifth of those infected developed pneumonia or septicaemia. Those hale and hearty at breakfast could be dead by tea time.

My father was an energetic man, and on moving to Wales became an agent for several manufacturers supplying the drapery trade. I remember as a youngster making deliveries with him in his pony and trap. But my father's agency in Wales was never a success – there were too many green fields and too few people. So before long the family moved back to Liverpool, where my father opened a new drapery business in Aintree, not far from the famous racecourse. It was a good move and the store did well. The shop was close to a farm, and in winter the farmer would flood one of his fields to provide the locals with a skating rink. I remember crawling through a hole in the hedge to get to the ice with one of my brothers –

'Where's your ticket?'

'Lost it.'

'Well don't do it again'.

But we did, and in truth spent many happy hours on the ice without paying a penny. There is no doubt about it, winters were colder in those days.

I was sent to Alsop High School. I was a reasonable scholar but

14

was hampered by ill health, particularly at exam time! I had a nasty bout of shingles, and even caught scarlet fever, another killer in those days. I spent six weeks in the Liverpool Isolation Hospital. There were rumours of a pauper's unmarked grave under the drive but I survived both the fever and the hospital.

In my teens I was disturbed when my mother Alice's health began to fail. I loved her dearly; she was a pretty and engaging woman, who would play cricket with us. I was sixteen at the time and my father took the family to Blackpool for a holiday but it didn't do my mother any good. She died a slow and painful death from breast cancer. The treatment for the disease in those days was horrific – the memory of those radium needles still makes me shudder. It had been my mother who held our family together, and after her death we drifted apart.

After school my father apprenticed me to a general store in Liverpool, and from there I drifted in and out of several jobs. I missed my mother and was something of a loner with little ambition. For a time I worked for my father, but that was a mistake. We were never close; he thought I was a hopeless salesman and uninterested in his business; of course he was right. What I wanted was to go to sea, but the timing was all wrong. It was at the height of the Depression and it seemed that half the people in Liverpool were out of work. My brother Roland had a master's ticket in the merchant navy but could only get a job as a quartermaster. When at last he found employment as an officer with the Malayan Steamship Company, the company was so short of money that it had cut its spending on food, relying on rough seas to dull passengers' appetites.

My father insisted that I remain in the retail trade. Roland backed him up, so I continued to drift from one employer to another. In the end I did find a job which I half liked, as an assistant at Lincoln Bennett, an upmarket retailer specialising in gentlemen's hats. Lincoln Bennett guaranteed its customers a perfect fit with its 'Conformatour'. It was a contraption used by us assistants to make an impression of individual heads so backroom staff could mould hard hats, bowlers and top hats to the right shape. There were strict rules; assistants were forbidden to ask customers for their hat size but were instructed to greet clients with a smile, offer them a cigarette and sit them in a comfortable chair. Most of our customers smoked and accepted the offer. We lost very few sales, and as a finishing touch we labelled each hat with our customers' initials. One of our rivals in the business used a different approach:

If in life you want to shine
Try one of ours at three and nine

For those of you younger than me, three shillings and nine pence is about 18 p.

In those days Battersby's of Stockport, Manchester, a leading hat manufacturer, introduced a new line, the 'Atta Boy'. The company was searching for ideas as to how they might market their new hat and put it to their workforce. There was one reply from the shop floor:

You can't be a Twat
In an Atta Boy Hat

The slogan was never used but it went the rounds and gave us a good laugh. Almost everybody between the wars wore hats or caps. They kept your head warm, and said something about you. A bowler indicated an up and coming businessman or foreman; a top hat told the world that you had arrived.

In the late twenties and early thirties thousands of Liverpool families faced real hardship. The poor would put anything on their heads to keep warm. But Liverpudlians were a tough lot, an extraordinary mixture of people from different countries and with different religions. Irish, Welsh, Scots, Blacks, Chinese, Poles, Greeks, Indians and Jews who knew about hard times and somehow survived. There was always tension in the city between Catholics and Protestants: brawls, fights and insults were the order of the day, but rarely murder. Somehow Catholic and Anglican priests managed to keep their flocks in some kind of order. They were helped by Catholics and Protestants living in adjoining streets, unlike in Belfast, where whole areas were segregated. Of course there were those on both sides who enjoyed confrontation and a fight, but there was often humour in the insults. A typical

Protestant chant was hardly life-threatening:

> *Catholic Catholic*
> *Quack Quack Quack*
> *Go to the Devil*
> *And don't come back*

And nowadays what has changed? The new Catholic cathedral is known as Paddy's Wigwam.

Oswald Moseley, leader of the Fascist party in the 1930s, thought that Liverpool would be a good recruiting ground. An enormous crowd turned out to meet him on his first visit to one of the poorest city suburbs; an open cart was used as a platform. Moseley was a rabble-rouser but had great presence and was a skilled orator. He soon had a crowd with him.

'Are you hungry?'

'Yes,' replied the crowd.

He repeated the question and the crowd roared.

'Then, friends,' said Moseley, 'there's a baker across the road, help yourselves.'

But Moseley hadn't done his homework. The Jewish bakery in question was known for giving free bread to those that needed it. There was a sudden change of mood. Moseley was booed, his cart upturned and he was lucky to make his escape. Somehow, most people managed to retain their sense of fairness and respect for what was right. Every week there would be a hunger march or demonstration. I felt sorry for the marchers, haggard and hopeless. There was something wrong with a country as rich as ours that couldn't find work for those that wanted it. But there was never any real danger that the fabric of society in Liverpool would break. Indeed the majority of those who lived in Liverpool were patriotic. As far as they were concerned 'Britannia ruled the waves' and to hell with the bloody Germans.

Despite the grinding poverty in Liverpool, which broke many families, there was always humour in the city streets and everyone looked forward to Guy Fawkes Night. Streets would vie with each other to build the largest bonfire, and come nightfall the bonfires in the poorest, narrowest street could be roof-high. A clear fire hazard.

The fire brigade did their best to keep the fires under control but were often thwarted by enthusiastic locals who roped off the streets or even sealed the fire hydrants.

Young and middle-aged women often caring for large families were known as 'Mary Ellens'. They dressed in a most distinctive fashion with large black shawls draped over their shoulders and fastened at the middle. The shawl formed a large pocket under each arm; often one would hold a baby, the other a bag and perhaps a little food which the Mary Ellen had managed to shoplift. Their men were known as Dicky Sams.

In the busy, bustling streets there were always ways of making some money, and a popular method was to hire a barrow and sell vegetables. Typically a Mary Ellen would hock her wedding ring for a barrow and a load of produce. Her cries were a feature of the city streets. At the end of the day she would have enough money to pay for the barrow and retrieve her ring.

Apples and pears, plums we have none
Sage and a bit of parsley, nice juicy oranges
White heather for luck young fella
Buy the last two and I'll give you three

It was not unusual for a barefoot youngster to approach a person eating an apple in the street – 'Give me the core mister!' Things were as bad as that.

Of course, not everyone in Liverpool was poor. Far from it. Liverpool, founded on sugar, rum, slavery and, later, cotton for England's industrial heartland, was still an extraordinarily rich city. For me the Liverpool waterfront was a source of wonder, and in my free time I was often drawn to it. There stood the Cunard buildings with great ships manoeuvring in the narrow river from all over the world: Canadian Pacific, the White Star Line, Cunarders and merchant ships, most flying the red ensign. Then there was the Mersey Overhead Railway, which covered miles of dockland with its modern electric trains, the service stretching over twenty-seven miles, such was the size of the docks. Underneath the overhead railway there were train lines for Puffing Billies that would ring a bell as they approached, and roadways for lorries, carts and horse-drawn vehicles. The docks were an exciting place, and the overhead railway was unique. What fools the Liverpool councillors were to tear it down when they redeveloped the city centre after the war. It was a marvellous asset and they couldn't see it.

Dockland was a great place to scrounge. There were spillages everywhere and the police were kept busy. Two small boys were seen stuffing their jackets and trousers with oranges from the quayside. A policeman caught them and locked them up in his station. After a few hours he let them out; there were no oranges to be seen.

'So,' said the policeman, 'you have eaten the evidence. You better go.'

'Yeah,' replied one of the boys as he ran off, 'and yer lunch.'

Against the background of poverty, children without shoes and with little to eat, the rich carried on much as they had before. The Liverpool Playhouse played to packed audiences, the restaurants and smart hotels had plenty of customers. Gentlemen in top hats and ladies dressed to kill were everywhere in the city centre. In the 1930s Liverpool became a centre of entertainment of every possible kind, with over three hundred places licensed for singing, dancing and variety shows. Leading opera and ballet companies would tour the city. And today, even though the city has changed beyond recognition and its docks almost gone, the theatrical tradition has continued – Ken Dodd with his Diddymen, his tickling stick, telling everyone about the Liverpool suburb Knotty Ash, Ted Ray, Jimmy Tarbuck, Arthur Askey, Cilla Black, the Liverpool Poets, the Spinners and of course the Beatles.

One day I was having yet another argument with my father about my future when he made a useful suggestion – 'Join the weekend sailors if you must.' And so it was that I joined the Royal Navy Volunteer Reserve Mersey Division as a boy seaman. On arrival at the RNVR headquarters in Liverpool docks, I was struck by an engraving on the training ship's bulkhead:

It is upon the Navy, under the providence of God, the safety of this Realm do chiefly depend

Under the engraving there was a splendid display of boarding pikes.

A real deterrent in sailing-ship days to those that might try and board one of His Majesty's Ships.

The Mersey Division was a much larger setup than I had imagined, with some eight hundred volunteers. The division had its own training ship, HMS *Eaglet*, a converted light cruiser which had seen action in the Battle of Jutland. I was delighted to be accepted and very proud when I was given the King's Shilling.[1] I should have kept it, but that evening I had a few beers with the chief yeoman who had interviewed me. The shilling was spent and I decided to become a signalman – or had the yeoman decided for me?

---

[1] In the seventeenth and eighteenth centuries a recruit to the army or navy would be given a shilling from the sovereign. Mersey Division had kept the tradition alive.

▲ Liverpool as I remember it in the late twenties – the Overhead Railway at the docks.

◄ The battle cruiser HMS *Renown*, which I joined in 1933, here follows immediately astern of her sister ship HMS *Repulse*, in the foreground of this picture of the fleet on exercise.

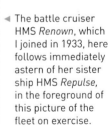

◄▲ HMS *Eaglet*, Mersey Division RNVR weekend training in 1936–37 (Clockwise from top left): rifle practice at Altcar, Lancashire; sailing dipping-lug cutters; rowing off the Point of Ayr, North Wales.

HMS *Leander*, first of a new class of cruiser, later assigned to the Royal New Zealand Navy.

◄ The battleship HMS *Nelson*.

The cruiser HMS *Adventure* – my ship from July 1939.

The Royal Yacht *Victoria and Albert* – much as she appeared during the Royal Fleet Reserve Review in August 1939.

▲ My pa, Quartermaster Sergeant Jones, of the Irby (Wirral) Home Guard.

▲ Senior Leading Firewoman Gladys Page.

▲ With my brothers Robert (centre), chief engineer with Bibby Line, and Roland (right), navigating officer on the Cunarder *Aquitania*.

◄ My brother Raymond in the army. As a Liverpool fireman, he was awarded a medal for saving an American soldier who fell into Bidston dock.

Roland brought the *Aquitania* into New York. We had two days together exploring the Big Apple.
▼

▲ *Adventure* had two escorting destroyers when she struck a mine in November 1939. HMS *Basilisk* came alongside at dawn to assist and took off the dead and injured. Our other escort HMS *Blanche* (above), was unlucky, as she too set off a mine and was sunk on the same morning. *Adventure,* thanks to calm seas and a tow, managed to limp back to port.

◀
German mine-layers in the North Sea. Some succeeded in getting right into the Thames estuary. The Royal Navy's minesweepers, including *Tritonia*, which I joined in January 1940, experimented with various methods before finding an effective way of dealing with magnetic mines. Floating electric cables towed astern would set them off at a safe distance.

▼ Lancing College, near Shoreham, where I took my officer training course.

▲ My first ship after being commissioned as a sub-lieutenant: HMS *Wastwater*. Sometimes referred to as one of the armed trawlers, she was in fact a Norwegian whaler.

◄ Exercising our 4-inch-gun crew. As gunnery officer, I was in charge of this Queen Victoria model – more danger to us than to the enemy, and useless against air attacks.

Ice from freezing spray is a serious winter hazard in the seas around Iceland and Greenland.

▼

The U-boat U-570, spotted on the surface, attacked and damaged by a Coastal Command Hudson, surrendered to the aircraft. Because of chlorine gas below decks, the crew would not leave the conning tower.

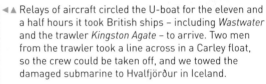

◀▲ Relays of aircraft circled the U-boat for the eleven and a half hours it took British ships – including *Wastwater* and the trawler *Kingston Agate* – to arrive. Two men from the trawler took a line across in a Carley float, so the crew could be taken off, and we towed the damaged submarine to Hvalfjörður in Iceland.

The U-boat was later towed to Britain, and recommissioned under the white ensign as HMS *Graph*.

Wreck of a merchant ship sunk by a U-boat off the coast of New Jersey after the USA entered the war in December 1941. *Wastwater* crossed the Atlantic to help protect US shipping. ▼

▲ First meal after reaching our US base at Staten Island, New York.

▲ F E Johnson's home at Peapack, New Jersey, where I enjoyed weekend breaks.

◄ Me in my American uniform. There was nothing left in our naval stores to fit me.

▲ The crew also enjoyed US hospitality.

◄ We escorted this floating dock from Boston to St Thomas in the West Indies. At three and a half knots we were sitting ducks. We made it, but the dock was later sunk on the way to Freetown.

▲ Passing Sail Rock, eastern extremity of the USA, on our way to the Caribbean.

Taking a sun shot. ▶

◀ Arriving at Santo Domingo.

▲ The crew go ashore.

▶

My British tropical whites, when they finally arrived, were most uncomfortable. Don't they look it?

◀ My first command, HMS *Baffin*, Admiralty trawler, in her dazzle paint. I joined her at Quebec.

▲ The officers of HMS *Baffin*. Lower right, next to me, is my first lieutenant, Archie Hodge.

◀ Friendly Indians. They worked at the steelworks in Sydney, Cape Breton Island.

▲ The harbour master catching seals on the ice.

▲ The inner harbour at Port aux Basques, Newfoundland. We escorted the old ferry, *Snaefell* (at the quay), which was brought out of retirement after the MS *Caribou* was torpedoed.

Baffin raising steam. ▶

▼ Home again in January 1944, Gladys and I get married.

◀ The trawler HMS *Guardsman* in Liverpool. I was her CO from March 1945.

▲ The King and Queen step ashore after their visit to *Guardsman* at Wallasey Dock.

◀▲ My very own U-boat. U-2334 surrenders to HMS *Guardsman* off Kristiansand, Norway.

▲ The minesweeper HMS *Bickington*, built in 1952, and attached to Sussex Division Royal Naval Reserve.

Officer of the watch. ▶

Lieutenant-commander's sleeve rings – attending the NCS course in Portsmouth.
▼

▲ The patrol boat HMS *Axford*, on a visit at Ostend.

Beginning a new career. My first year form at Portslade County Secondary School for boys, where I taught 1948–55.
▼

2

At last I go to sea – and on a battle cruiser

In the autumn of 1933 I went to sea for the first time – two weeks' sea training in HMS *Renown*, a 26,500 ton battle cruiser. A party of us had been sent by train to join the ship at Invergordon. The *Renown* had been launched in 1916 and joined the North Sea Fleet just a few weeks after the great Battle of Jutland. Six months earlier and she could have been Admiral Beatty's flagship. The *Renown* was second only to the *Hood* as the pride of the Royal Navy and carried the Prince of Wales on his world tour. But when I joined her all that remained of that jolly was a badminton court.

I had never been away from home before and I marvelled at the great ship's size, its order and routine, and the ceremonial, which included the Royal Marine band beating retreat and then taking up their fiddles to play at a captain's dinner. On board I caught many a glimpse of the old Navy, beginning with the bosun's shrill pipe which wakened us at 0545 with the time-honoured call, 'Wakey, wakey rise and shine, lash up and stow.' Within minutes we would be out of our hammocks – one of the few pieces of kit Nelson would have recognised – and our bedding stowed. I never had any difficulty in sleeping in a hammock, which is surprisingly comfortable. Then again, by the end of the day I was so tired that I could have slept on a board.

The early morning calls were not without humour and would change from time to time. One favourite was:

Wakey wakey, rise and shine.
You've had your time, now I'll have mine.

And then there was another old chestnut:

Wakey wakey, rise and shine.
The morning's fine. Rig of the day, oilskins.

I was astonished by the number of crew on the *Renown*. There were men everywhere, including a number of three-badge seamen – older men, some of whom had marvellous ditty boxes. These were carved and decorated boxes in which seamen kept their personal and most private possessions. It was an unwritten law that nobody would ever meddle with another man's box.

I was on board for *Renown*'s autumn shoot. A battered old warship, HMS *Conquest*, was towed out of harbour to act as a decoy. The shoot itself was a spectacular affair, the noise deafening. Star shells illuminated the target, guns flashed and smoke billowed from the cordite. The ship shook itself like a dog after each salvo. Most of the ship's company had no sight of what was happening, but as a trainee signalman I had a perfect view from the back of the bridge. From there it seemed, despite all the noise and effort, there were many misses and few hits. There was no explosive in the shells, and at the end of the shoot the decoy was towed back to the harbour, battered but fit for another day's shoot.

Throughout training we didn't have a moment to ourselves, apart from Sunday afternoon, which was free time. By then we needed a break because in some respects Sunday morning was the most stressful part of the week. At 1000 there would be divisions, followed by a church service on the quarter deck and after that captain's rounds. The leading seaman in charge of our mess insisted that it be immaculate in every respect, and we ourselves a credit to him. A collar with the tiniest of marks would have to be rewashed. Our mess kits were laid out on our table, every piece polished and re-polished until they gleamed. At 1130 the captain, proceeded by a marine bugler and followed by his heads of departments, swept into our mess. The captain spoke to our leading seaman, smiled and was gone.

'He seems to be in a hurry,' I whispered to a two-badge seaman.

'Aye, he's looking forward to his drinks and a slap-up luncheon while we get our dinner.'

On the Monday training would continue at a frantic pace. 'Raise the anchor by hand' was a regular evolution. Wooden bars were inserted into the large capstan on the forecastle and manned by four men to each bar. On the command a lone fiddler would start to play as the men pushed their bars, the capstan revolving and pulling the anchor chain and finally the anchor on board. Other evolutions followed in quick succession – 'Rig a collision mat port bow! Put out a fire in the port waist! Action stations, action stations, prepare for aircraft attack! All sea boats away! Five men overboard port quarter!' and so it went on. One day there was a real surprise when we were told to re-enact the mutiny of the Nore. We sailors were the mutineers and were sent ashore. An hour later the marines landed, firing guns, and the chase began. Everybody had a good time, and by 1200 the mutineers were duly caught and shot and it was all over. No one, mutineer or marine, wanted to miss their tot or their dinner.

There was a lot to learn on such a big ship, not least the ability to find one's way from one part to another: Where to find one's cleaning station, an entering and leaving harbour station, an action station. But the one place we were never allowed, except for the Sunday church service, was the quarter deck. It was from the quarter deck, guarded by marine sentries, that the routine of the ship was controlled. The officers, and the quartermaster with his pipe, would be immaculate, and the sailors too as smart as could be managed; the deck so clean that it seemed a crime for us ordinary ratings to walk on it. It was on the quarter deck where foreign dignitaries and other ship's captains would be received, such ceremonious occasions choreographed to the minutest detail. The bosun would pipe and a body of marines present arms. One day I caught a glimpse of the wardroom (the officers' mess), another no-go area. It was rather grand and in some respects like a London club except that there were old magazines instead of daily newspapers, and there was strict protocol on how officers should behave.

As a raw recruit I was full of wonder. It seemed that everybody on board lived in a world within a world, cut off from the reality of everyday life. But somehow, without consciously knowing it, I sensed and followed the unwritten rules of how I should behave.

Lieutenant Hugh Mulleneux, RN, an officer serving on the *Renown*, 'Meux' to his friends. He had his son Peter christened on *Renown*, and sprinkled with holy water from the upturned ship's bell. After the war Lieutenant Peter Mulleneux would serve with me at the Sussex Division RNVR.

On *Renown* the captain's word was law, and beyond him there was a wide divide between officers and ratings. All-powerful on their own ships, captains were nevertheless expected to obey, without question, the orders of their superior officers. I was a keen reader of naval history and there was an argument that had more initiative been granted to the captains of the ships actually fighting the Battle of Jutland the British could have won an outright victory. 'There is the enemy,' Nelson would have said, 'engage more closely!' But alas our battle fleet was ordered to turn away from the enemy at a critical moment and the German fleet escaped.

Now there were many talented officers in the *Renown*. The wardroom was populated by experts in every field. Doctors, engineers, writers, wireless specialists, dentists, gunners, humorists, and the most marvellous cartoonists. And in the mess decks too there were skilled engineers in every discipline, musicians, singers, engravers and brilliant seamen. It would seem to be an almost ideal life. But it is too easy to romanticise. Living on a battleship for two years or more, with its strict routine, separated from family, home and friends, could become dull, tiresome and stressful. Many a good man drank too much. Nevertheless, to serve on such a ship was a great privilege. Years later, I met a young RNVR officer who had been christened on that great and beautiful battle cruiser in 1934. His father was a ship's gunnery officer. The ship's bell was turned upside down, the water made holy and Master Peter Mulleneux was christened by the ship's chaplain. After which there was a splendid party, and young Peter's name was inscribed on the bell.

But I digress – back to the young recruits. We were like rabbits, scurrying from one part of the *Renown* to another. But large as she was, our ship was nothing like the size of some of the modern-day American carriers, with a crew of five thousand and operational aircraft. Those great ships fill me with wonder.

One thing that I still remember about the *Renown* was the difficulty in understanding what seemed an entirely new language. Sailors spoke to each other in a shorthand of swear words, but cut through that was humour and understanding. I picked up a poem from one of the older men:

I was walking through the dockyard in a panic
When I met a matelot old and grey.
On his back he had his kitbag and his hammock
And this is what I heard him say,
'Oh I wonder, yes I wonder
Did the jaunty make a blunder
When he made this draft chit out for me?
A million miles I've travelled
And a million sites I've seen
And I always said good morning to the Chief,
I've dwelt in barrack stations
And Aggie Weston's mansions
And now they're sending me to sea.
Oh I wonder, yes I wonder
Did the jaunty make a blunder
When he made this draft chit out for me?'

It's not much of a poem, but it manages to capture the life, the regret and the loneliness of an old seaman finishing his time. And in the 1920s and 30s there were thousands of such men. In those days most ports had their Aggie Westons, where sailors, for a few shillings a night, could get a clean bed free from lice and a nourishing breakfast.[2]

The year after my sea training on *Renown* I was drafted to HMS *Leander*. *Leander* was a light cruiser but with her six-inch guns and other armament she packed a punch. She was very fast and had a speed of over thirty-two knots. For a few minutes while I was on board we steamed at near maximum revs. That was a great thrill, and the mountain of sea astern was something to marvel at.

My time on *Leander* passed quickly. I felt at home and I think the officers and the ship's yeomen were impressed at how much I

---

[2] Aggie Weston (1840–1918) realised that sailors needed a safe haven when ashore and set up a series of hostels in many of the major ports. The first of the Royal Sailors' Rests was opened in association with the Royal Navy Temperance Society in 1876 in Fore Street, Devonport, near the Plymouth Royal Dockyard. Engraved on the window was the legend 'Coffee, comfort, and company for One Penny'.

had learnt in two short years. Nevertheless, I was surprised when the captain recommended me for officer training. Had my energetic polishing of the brass tags on the flag hoists made an impression? The captain had seemed pleased; the chief yeoman anything but.

'Why did you do such a silly thing?' he asked.

'Well, you told me to polish something.'

He sighed. 'And who's going to polish the bloody things next week?'

'Sorry chief.'

But the yeoman shook my hand and gave me a smile when my two weeks were up.

On a training evening a few weeks later the captain of HMS *Mersey*, a Captain RN, asked to see me. Gently, he told me that he had my application for officer training but thought it was not the right time.

'Look,' he said, 'you will never be able to afford it. Derby and his friends spend their money as if there is no tomorrow. They run the wardroom like a private club – dinners, dances, receptions and God knows what else. I must tell you, Jones,' he added rather bitterly, 'that I find it difficult to pay my way.'

So it was agreed that he would put my application on one side.

'I am sure things will change' said the captain, 'and then we will reconsider. I am so sorry.'

It was strange. I didn't mind, and soon forgot about being an officer. I was happy to be a signalman – it was after all the Navy's crack branch. But the incident showed how strong the class system was in those days.

From 1935 onwards it was obvious, despite what some politicians were telling us, that the country was heading for war. There were many in Liverpool who didn't care; anything was better than being on the dole. Slowly there was more work, and then, almost overnight, the shipbuilders had full order books. And my family, all in their own ways, were themselves preparing for an uncertain future. Following the death of my mother Alice my father had married my mother's best friend. I didn't blame him or her, but sometimes, living in different digs around Liverpool, I was lonely and perhaps a little depressed. I saw little of my three brothers, who were pursuing their own careers, but we remained good friends and whenever one of Roland's ships came into Liverpool we would try and meet up. One evening he introduced me to Charles Herbert Lightoller, DSC, who was the senior officer to survive the sinking of the *Titanic* and who had been decorated for gallantry during the First World War.[3] He was a tall, wiry man with a nice smile and I liked him.

I continued my unsatisfactory jobs in retail, but spent every spare moment with the RNVR, which had become my life. I volunteered for everything – sailing weekends, the guard of honour and the field gun crew. For three years my annual training was spent at HMS *Drake*, the Royal Navy Signal School in Devonport, where I enjoyed my time, and at the end, although I say it myself, I was a competent signalman.

As a member of the HMS *Mersey* guard of honour I witnessed two great occasions: in 1937 the launch of the HMS *Ark Royal*, the celebrated aircraft carrier that did so much in the early stages of the war; and in the spring of 1939 the launch of the battleship *Prince of Wales*. Thousands turned out to cheer and emotions ran high. Many of us felt that our navy would give the Huns a bloody good hiding and the sooner we started the better. It was unimaginable that within three years both these fine ships would be sunk by our enemies, with great loss of life.

It was a coincidence that the Officer of Guard was a Lieutenant Bennett-Jones. He was no relation, and although a reserve officer wore full ceremonial dress, a frock coat and a cocked hat of the kind Nelson might have worn. We became good friends despite him being an officer and me being an ordinary signalman. He was a good man, and I am pleased to have a picture of us both at the launch of *Princess of Wales*. I

---

[3] At the age of thirteen Commander C H Lightoller began a four-year seagoing apprenticeship on sailing ships. He was shipwrecked on an uninhabited island, and on another trip the cargo of coal caught fire. This was not unusual in those days. He left the sea in 1898 to prospect for gold in the Klondike. Unsuccessful, he became a cowboy in Canada; but in 1900 he joined the White Star Line, and later sailed on the *Titanic*'s maiden voyage. His heroism in saving as many passengers as possible from the sinking ship was portrayed by Kenneth More in the film *A Night to Remember*. In June 1940, with his eldest son Roger, he sailed his boat the *Sundowner* to Dunkirk. Although his small ship had never carried more than 21 people he saved 130 men from the beaches.

The Princess Royal Inspecting the guard of honour at Birkenhead in 1937 before the launch of the *Prince of Wales*. The Officer of the Guard is in full ceremonial uniform and I am in there under the white arrow.

am one of those sailors in the front rank, and my friend is wearing his magnificent hat.

In 1938 I was drafted for two weeks' sea training to HMS *Nelson*, a battleship and flagship of the home fleet. It was a disappointment to find *Nelson* in Devonport in dry dock under repair. I remember the extraordinary time it took to walk across the ship's gangways to shore for a pee and then back to the ship for another class. God knows what one did if caught short. I reckon to have walked miles during those two weeks. No ship looks its best in dry dock, and while HMS *Nelson* was very powerful, with its massive 16-inch guns named after the seven dwarfs (Grumpy, Happy, Dopey, Doc, etc.), it was an ugly duckling of a ship. It had been built under the constraints of the Washington Naval Treaty of 1922, which stipulated a maximum tonnage of 35,000 tons. There had to be compromises: the ship's planned length was shortened and her speed reduced, and consequently she could be difficult to handle. What Nelson thought of his new ship I had no idea, but he was on board – his uniform was kept in a glass case near the wardroom together with a lock of his hair. And what did he think of the Portsmouth Harbour incident? The first time his new battleship left Portsmouth Harbour it grounded on Hamilton Bank. 'Once again Nelson mounts Hamilton,' was how a popular newspaper described the incident.

The salute of nineteen guns for the visit of the First Lord of the Admiralty to Liverpool, and taking the guns with fellow members of the RNVR to the Albert Parade. Once again I was there, not that you can see much of me – look for the arrow.

I was astonished to find that there were over forty signalmen on *Nelson*. I could not understand why so many were needed. Perhaps it was the normal entitlement for a flagship, but there was a design fault. Officers on the bridge could not see the flag deck, and the signal staff could not see the bridge. It was a strange couple of weeks but the training was good and I got to spend a few days at sea on destroyers working up. On the bright side, Plymouth was a good place for a run ashore – by then I knew my way around.

HMS *Nelson* survived the war, but only just, and spent a considerable time under repair and in harbour. At a speed of twenty knots she was too slow to catch the German pocket battleships in the North Sea, and in 1940 she struck a magnetic mine off the Scottish coast. Nobody was hurt but the damage was extensive, and it was over six months before she could be repaired and rejoin the fleet. By then I knew a thing or two about the new German mines, which posed a real threat to our navy and our country.

As usual, after time with the Navy, it was an anticlimax to return to Liverpool and Lincoln Bennett. 'Would you like a cigarette sir?

Please sit down and make yourself comfortable' – O God, the very thought of it. To hell with the Conformatour! But this time it would be little more than a few months before the balloon went up.

We knew in Liverpool that Prime Minister Chamberlain's advice to the British people that there would be 'peace in our time' was tosh, and we had not long to wait. In July 1939 the Mersey Division was mobilised and sent off to man the reserve fleet. Most of the Mersey Division ratings were marched to the station with our kit bags on our shoulders. Nobody cheered and little was said – we were venturing into the unknown. The train took us to Devonport in Plymouth and the mobilisation was extraordinarily efficient. Of course there was a medical examination, with lines of us, half-naked, waiting in a queue, but quickly we were allocated to different ships and given our duties, our mess and our action stations. Nothing was left to chance.

3

War

Medical inspection over, a petty officer handed me my joining papers.

'You are off to an Adventure,' he joked. 'She's a cruiser.'

'Leander class?' I asked, excited at the prospect.

'No, she's a minelayer. Not much of a job for a cruiser but I'm sure you'll get on.'

When not working up off Plymouth, we spent as much time as possible painting and cleaning HMS *Adventure*. There was plenty to do, as the ship had been manned on a care-and-maintenance basis for the past three years. On 2 August we sailed for Weymouth, where the reserve fleet was being assembled for a royal fleet review.

On Wednesday 9 August 1939, 133 ships were anchored in Weymouth Bay. It was a foggy, misty morning; the ships looked like grey ghosts on the water. Slowly the Royal Yacht, the *Victoria and Albert*, with King George VI on board, sailed past the anchored warships.[4] The yacht with its big yellow funnels and three masts looked something of museum piece, but with her flags fluttering she was impressive enough. As she approached, the crew of each ship manned the sides and cheered as she came close to them. As she sailed past *Adventure*, I found that there were tears in my eyes; being a signalman I had a better view than most. At that time King George VI personally

---

[4] The *Victoria & Albert*, launched in 1899 and commissioned in 1901, had been built after Queen Victoria lobbied Parliament for a new royal yacht, pointing out that both the Russian Tsar and the German Kaiser had larger and more modern yachts.

owned more ships than anybody else in the world, but he must have wondered how many of his old, trusted and sometimes rusty vessels would survive another war. But for all that it was an impressive occasion, and perhaps more importantly, 12,000 reservists had increased the manpower of the Royal Navy to 160,000 men.

After the review there was a quiet period; it seemed that we might be sent home. Had our king inspecting his reserve fleet made Hitler change his mind? We soon had the answer. War was declared on 3 September. I never heard Chamberlain's speech but the news was broadcast over the ship's tannoy. It was strange. Most of us just accepted the fact and thought little more about it. On the bright side, my career in retailing was over. And for us, on the *Adventure*, the outbreak of war was something of an anticlimax. We didn't go to sea and start fighting the Germans – quite the reverse, the ship's company was given seven days' leave and I went home to Liverpool.

For the most part I enjoyed my time on the ship. The work of a qualified signalman was interesting, and I had a degree of freedom which was not given to most ratings. I was happy enough – I had a place to sling my hammock, the ship had a good cook, and my cleaning station was just one flight of steps to the bridge, the captain's personal gangway. My abandon-ship station was a Carley float on the port waist. It was there that I asked the petty officer in charge whether the one Carley float would be sufficient for the forty-odd ratings who had mustered.

'Don't worry lad, half of you will be dead before we abandon ship.'

There was one problem, though. The commander, a Royal Naval officer, had made it clear that he didn't like reservists on his ship. Reason enough to be nervous – and then, a couple of days

'Defaulters' – a cartoon produced in the wardroom of HMS *Renown*

before the review, idly walking along the beach while on shore leave I had kicked a stone. How was I to know that the commander's silly dog would chase it and in so doing knock over his wife's cup of tea? The following day I was in a line of defaulters waiting to see the commander, facing a charge that my behaviour had been prejudicial to the good order and discipline of the Royal Navy. I could see from the gleam in the commander's eye that he was still angry. There was nothing for it – I made a grovelling apology.

'Case dismissed!' he barked, but continued to call me out whenever he had the chance.

Four weeks later we were bound for Rosyth in Scotland. It was a grey misty morning and while we were steaming underneath the Forth Bridge – almost a wonder of the world for some of us – a German plane, its markings clear, came out of the clouds immediately above us. 'Action stations, action stations!' I was on the bridge, and rushed down a ladder to the signal distribution office while on another ladder the commander rushed to the bridge.

'What are you doing, Jones?' he barked.

'My action stations, sir, the SDO.'

He grunted – he thought I was running away. The German plane disappeared into the clouds. I guess he was almost as surprised to see us as we were to see him. It was the third week of the war.

Still, strained relations with the commander aside I was popular on board. Oddly, I had my father to thank for that, as with my draper's training I could alter uniforms, hats, flags and shore clothing. I even made a new cap for our surgeon lieutenant, who had been promoted.

Adventure's first and most important task after the outbreak of war was to help lay a mine barrage off the Goodwin Sands, which was extended to the French coast. In a few days three thousand mines were laid so that by the end of October there was no safe passage for U-boats through the Straits of Dover. The task was made easier by the Admiralty commandeering two cross-channel ferries with railway tracks, ideal for the job.

In November, disaster. I nearly lost my life. The *Adventure* struck a German magnetic mine in the Thames Estuary. Our ship was badly damaged. Sixteen were killed, mostly petty officers, and more than sixty injured, some seriously. I was asleep when the mine exploded. I woke in inky darkness. I'd been blown right out of my hammock through a doorway and into a flat. There was a great deal of noise and the terrible sound of a man screaming.

'For Christ's sake, don't strike a match!' a petty officer shouted. He was right, of course – there could well have been gas or cordite in the air which could go up in a flash. It was some time before a torch was found and we were able to see where we were. The ship had keeled over by some fifteen degrees, but to us it seemed like fifty. At first we thought the hatch above us had been battened down. It was a bad moment. Once a damaged compartment is battened down, it's not opened until the ship docks; opening could mean the loss of the ship. We pushed our shoulders to the offending hatch and thanked God when it opened. At some point in the darkness and the chaos I gripped a steam pipe, burning my hand, but at the time I didn't feel the pain. Opening the hatch we hauled ourselves through to the next deck and passed up two injured men. It seemed a long time as we groped along the passage to the next ladder. On the way we passed a closed hatch which led down to the stoker petty officers' mess. I didn't like to think how many were down there and hoped that some of them were still alive.

Finally we reached the upper deck on the starboard side; it was crowded with all hands. Everyone was calm. Messengers, damage control squads and stretcher parties were reporting and moving off. The injured men were being treated on the main deck, where a number of corpses had been hung over the lifeline like towels on a rail. There was no time to clean up the blood that dripped from the corpses. Still half-dressed, I reported to the bridge.

In addition to those that had been killed we had a large number of casualties. The mine had set off one of our magazines, and such was the force of the two explosions that some of those on deck and even on the bridge had their legs broken. One poor man, dead, was pinioned to a deck head.

All this happened in the dark, but there was no panic. At daybreak one of the *Adventure*'s escorting destroyers, HMS *Basilisk*, came alongside and took off many of the wounded, leaving a volunteer party on board to try and save the ship. I volunteered to stay as my injuries were minor, I wasn't married and the ship was

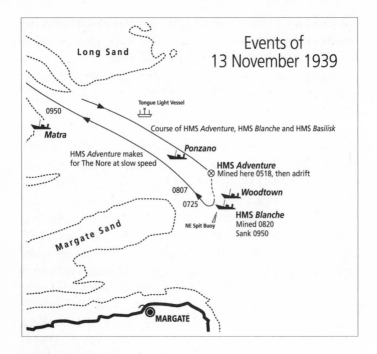

Events of
13 November 1939

Long Sand

0950

Matra

Tongue Light Vessel

Course of HMS *Adventure*, HMS *Blanche* and HMS *Basilisk*

Ponzano

HMS *Adventure* makes
for The Nore at slow speed

HMS *Adventure*
⊗ Mined here 0518, then adrift

0807

Woodtown

0725

NE Spit Buoy

HMS *Blanche*
Mined 0820
Sank 0950

Margate Sand

MARGATE

short of signalmen. Indeed, for some time, before being joined by just one watch officer, I was the only man on the bridge.

I spent the rest of the day – and it was a long day – on the bridge. Almost all the instruments were shattered, and all I could find to signal with was one box Aldis lamp. It was a misty morning, and the officer of the watch asked me if I could see our escorting destroyer, HMS *Blanche*. I found her with my telescope and then before my eyes she disappeared. She had sunk, a German mine had got her too. Partly under her own steam, *Adventure* was towed into dock. It was fortunate the weather held, as she would surely have sunk in any kind of a sea. We didn't know it at the time but as it transpired there was a hole in the *Adventure*'s bottom through which you could have driven a bus. By the end of the day, still dressed in little more than a singlet, I felt cold, shivery and out of sorts. The medical officer, seeing my distress, lent me his spare jacket but the commander was having none of it.

'Why are you wearing that jacket, Jones? Take it off.'

The medical officer rolled his eyes, but the commander, an

officer of the old school and one with no regard for reservists, was not open to question.

When we got to barracks I looked remarkably well, and despite my injured hand had a problem in persuading the officer in charge to grant survivor's leave. Suddenly, without warning, I passed out. Delayed shock, I suppose.

As a result of this shaky and explosive start to my war I was sent to a naval hospital where we were all dressed in blue uniforms. There were regular service-type inspections and we were stood to attention lying in a bed or sitting in a chair. In hospital I could not help but remember the sad story of a young rating who had to have his appendix removed by the ship's surgeon. By chance *Adventure* had to call in at Hartlepool, the rating's home town. Thoughtfully the surgeon had asked his mother and father to come on board and see him. Of course the parents had been delighted by the surgeon's suggestion that they take him home and look after him until he was better. But the sailor was having none of it. 'I'll stay with the ship,' he told them firmly. Three days later *Adventure* struck the mine and he was dead.

After a week I was discharged from hospital and went home to Liverpool on sick leave. One day, sitting on a bus, the conductor came up to me.

'I see you was on the *Adventure*.'

I was surprised, but then remembered I was in uniform.

'Atkins was a friend of mine.'

Atkins? And then I remembered the body pinioned to the deck head.

I was at home when I heard about the Battle of the River Plate.[5]

---

[5] The Battle of the River Plate was one of the most famous naval battles of the Second World War despite involving only four ships. Two Leander class light cruisers (*Ajax* and *Achilles*) and a York class heavy cruiser (*Exeter*) took on the *Admiral Graf Spee*, a German pocket battleship – on the face of it an unequal contest, with the British cruisers having six-inch and eight-inch guns and the *Graf Spee* eleven-inch. But the three British captains knew what to do, approaching the *Graf Spee* from three different quarters. The *Exeter* was badly damaged but so was the *Graf Spee*, which was forced to put into Montevideo to carry out some emergency repairs. The German Captain, Langsdorff, decided to scuttle his ship rather than face another battle. He then committed suicide.

The defeat of the *Graf Spee* was regarded as a great victory. At last there was something to celebrate, and I could tell my friends that I had once served on a Leander class cruiser.

I didn't have to wait long for my next draft. It was to the key naval base in Orkney, Scapa Flow. However, once again I was not destined for a great ship, but one HMS *Tritonia*, a minesweeper, a converted herring drifter. She was part of a squadron involved in sweeping safe channels for our ships and, just as important, in finding an antidote for the new German magnetic mines which had so nearly sunk *Adventure*. Many of the trawler minesweepers were skippered by men who had fished from them in peacetime. I joined the *Tritonia* at Lowestoft and then, for some reason, we sailed to Liverpool. Alas, the *Tritonia* was not the kind of ship I could boast about to my friends, but at least she flew the White Ensign. A week later we sailed for Scapa and once there I was kept busy. Signalmen were in short supply and I was often sent from one ship to another. Scapa is one of the greatest natural harbours in the world, and is where Germany surrendered its High Seas Fleet at the end of the First World War.[6]

But when *Tritonia* arrived at Scapa, with the exception of our minesweeping squadron it was almost deserted, and no wonder. In October 1939, just after the outbreak of war, a daring U-boat commander, Captain Prien, had breached the harbour's defences and torpedoed the battleship *Royal Oak* with great loss of life, including a hundred boy seamen. This was not just a disaster for the Royal Navy but a propaganda victory for the German U-boats. In the ensuing panic and in a great hurry the harbour defences had been strengthened by grounding two merchantmen in the narrow channel round Holm Island, but in the rush the ships' papers had been left on board. One of our first tasks was to go alongside the two ships and retrieve the documents. It was a wet and messy business.

---

[6] The natural harbour of Scapa Flow in Orkney has been used as an anchorage since Viking times. It was the main base of the Royal Navy in both World Wars, and the last port of call for the German High Seas Fleet, which scuttled in its waters. The wreckage left is a reminder of one of the greatest moments in British maritime history. Orkney is blessed with clean waters and an abundance of marine life. On a fine day it is one of the most wonderful places in the world.

Tritonia was skippered by an extraordinary and likable man. Born to command, Danny Smith was barely five feet tall, so he had had a herring box installed on the bridge so he could stand on it and see what was going on. For some reason there was no end of paint on the ship, so one day I asked the captain if he would like me to brighten things up a bit. He agreed and I set to work, painting the bridge, his cabin, the wheelhouse and whatever else took my fancy. Danny was delighted, and took to showing my efforts to other ships' captains.

At first I was surprised by the seeming lack of discipline in our squadron. It was not unknown for a whole ship's company to go ashore leaving their minesweeper with just the ship's cat in charge. For the most part no one bothered much about uniform unless going on leave or entering a new port. Then uniforms were often illegally embellished with a gunner's badge, or even a signalman's – 'The girls love a uniform, and the more badges the better.'

In the spring of 1940 the weather improved but the news from home was grim. We were a self-contained unit and took little notice of what was happening elsewhere. For days on end we hardly listened to the BBC. But now suddenly it appeared that our army in France was in desperate straits. All leave was cancelled with all ships put on standby to sail for the English Channel. I was on deck when a launch with an army sergeant in charge drew alongside.

'These are for you,' he said, and handed me a heavy box half full of Mills bombs.

'What are we to do with them?' I asked.

'Throw them at the enemy, of course.'

'If we can get close enough,' I replied, amused at the thought. But by then he was off delivering his bombs to other ships of our squadron. We continued to listen to the news and realised how dire the situation was when the King and the Archbishop of Canterbury ordered a week of prayer. In the end, the defeat at Dunkirk, although grievous in every way, was turned into an act of divine deliverance. We, however, could never have got to Dunkirk in time, and the next day our sailing instructions were cancelled.

One incident raised our spirits. One of our Tribal class destroyers had captured a German minelayer, *Piroc*, and escorted it into our base. It was good to see crestfallen German prisoners taken ashore, and much to our delight we found extra food and drink on the enemy ship. Also, and much more important, the Germans had left one of their new magnetic mines on deck. Immediately a signal was sent to HMS *Vernon*, the mine school in Portsmouth, and within hours two boffins arrived.

My captain asked me in a casual manner if I would mind going over to the captured German minelayer and assisting the two experts from *Vernon*.

'It would be useful if you could keep in touch with us by signal,' he added.

'Of course sir,' I replied. What else could I say?

I was a bit suspicious when *Tritonia* kept well clear of the German minelayer. Did my captain expect the worst? Had he an idea that the enterprise would fail? As it happened, the thread of the German screws on the mine was opposite to the thread of screws made in England. After a series of bangs, crashes and curses from the two experts I began to feel nervous – even more so when they asked me to signal for help. Our chief engineer from the *Tritonia* identified the problem but didn't hang around. He was in and out of *Piroc* in minutes. It was a very long day before the deed was done.

It came as a complete surprise when a little later I was told that my captain and the squadron electrical officer James had recommended me for the Distinguished Service Medal. Not only that – Danny, God bless him, recommended me for officer training.

Later that summer there was an outbreak of German measles. Always susceptible to any kind of infection, I was one of the first to catch it. Immediately I was put into isolation, which meant I was confined with one other sufferer to a small cabin, little more than a hut, on the shore. When he thought about it, and that was by no means every day, a doctor would look in at us. Apart from that and a rather erratic delivery of food from the next-door village, we were left to ourselves. With nothing to do, and feeling better, we took to going for walks and once, greatly daring, we rowed across a creek and purchased a bottle of whisky from a pub. It cost seven shillings and six pence, quite a sum, but it helped no end with our convalescence. Just three days later my new friend was pronounced free from infection and sufficiently recovered to resume his normal duties. Three days later I followed him.

4

I go back to school and meet Gladys

Before I could become a CW candidate (an officer cadet) I had to pass an Admiralty Board. I was interviewed by four officers, all fairly covered with gold braid. They congratulated me on my Distinguished Service Medal and asked a few gentle questions.

'Why are you not wearing your decoration?' enquired the most senior of the officers.

'Well,' I said, 'I didn't like to do that before being given it.'

'Really? I put up mine right away.' He had a chest full of medals.

'What games do you play?' asked another.

'Cricket', I replied, 'and football.'

There was a silence.

'And I like riding,' I added.

'So you're a horseman,' said the chairman, 'that's splendid'.

'No, sir, I was a member of the East Liverpool Cycling Club.'

Nevertheless the Board recommended me for officer training.

So, at the age of twenty-six, it was back to school, this time to Lancing College. By the time I arrived, however, it was no longer Lancing College, but HMS *King Alfred*, a training school for young naval officers. The college, with its cloisters and soaring chapel, had become a remarkable stone frigate (naval slang for a shore station). In three short months most of us would indeed become officers, something that would previously have taken years.

A few days after the Board a number of us were driven to Lancing. It was late in the evening when the bus slowly climbed the hill to the school. Out of the darkness its chapel loomed above us. I had never seen anything like it. 'Abandon hope, all ye who enter here,' I said to myself. We got off the bus. It was very cold and windy and the place seemed deserted.

Finally a duty officer appeared. 'Divisions are at 0800. Make sure you're not late and smarten up!'

We were shown to a cold, echoing dormitory. What was the Navy thinking of to send us to such a place, I thought, as I struggled to get to sleep.

The next morning everything was transformed. There was a cheerful bustle about the place and we were given an excellent breakfast, although we had great trouble waking Robert, an ex-customs officer, who was still half asleep when we eventually coaxed him out onto the parade ground. There were at least two hundred men on parade. I wondered where they had all come from. Each morning a different cadet took charge – it was a nerve-wracking experience. The parades were under the strict control of Chief Petty Officer Vass, a gunner.

One cadet, overcome by the experience, failed to give the final order to prevent his men marching off the parade ground.

'Say something lad,' said CPO Vass, 'even if it is only goodbye.'

The cadets at Lancing were an extraordinary mixture, some with little sea experience. The majority, who in twelve short weeks would become officers, were from the lower deck. In those days there was a huge divide between officers and men. 'It will never work,' said some, but it did, and *King Alfred* trained and promoted over twenty thousand men; it was a social experiment on a grand scale. We were kept busy, with lessons in boat-handling, gunnery, signalling, wireless, torpedoes, code books, navigation, even knots and splices. The syllabus was vast, the tuition excellent. While all this was going on we were being turned into officers – how to behave at dinners (it's not a serviette, it's a napkin), at receptions and in a wardroom. Some keen cadets, known as Sherries, would take sherry before dinner, but I stuck with the gin.

It wasn't just training. At times it was for real. Brighton, in 1941, was to some extent on the front line. German bombers failing to find their target used the town as a dumping ground, sometimes causing heavy loss of life. One day during boat drill at Shoreham Harbour a German plane swooping down Aldrington Basin towards the gas station sprayed a few bullets. 'Damn near hit me,' said the petty officer in charge.

I must tell you how I met Gladys. I was anxious to see Brighton, and most evenings there was a liberty bus which ran from the college to central Brighton. There was a strict instruction that all cadets must catch the return bus at 2300. Some places were out of bounds, and in particular a club at the bottom of West Street. We knew the reason why. Usually Bob, the sleepy customs officer, and I hit the town together.

One evening we went to the Regent Ballroom and Picture House, near the clock tower where Boots now stands. While I was at the bar I was astonished to see Bob dancing with the best-looking girl in the ballroom. You're far too good for him, I thought, and at the next 'excuse me' I took over. It was not long before I had fallen in love with Gladys, but I didn't tell her, not right away. Perhaps it was fortunate that my friend Bob was taken ill and hospitalised in Mowden. The competition was out of the way – I had Gladys to myself. Nevertheless, when Bob recovered he passed his course and we remained friends.

Life in the college carried on and I enjoyed myself. Singing together in the magnificent chapel was a joy, and the companionship and good humour of my fellow cadets was infectious. Our instructors made it clear they were there to help. The days flashed by and Gladys, God bless her, was living in Brighton, just over the hill.

In February I was given two days' leave to go to London to meet the king at Buckingham Palace. He, personally, was to give me my Distinguished Service Medal. That was a great honour. Waiting in the corridor to enter the ballroom where the investiture was to be held, I asked if there was a toilet. 'Certainly sir,' replied a very polite attendant, who showed me to a very long narrow room. At the end of the room there was just one pink toilet, with a chain hanging from the ceiling.

In the ballroom a band played, and the king stood on a dais. I was given my instructions: 'When you approach the king, you stop and bow. He will shake you by the hand. He may talk to you before giving you your medal. You then walk three paces backwards and bow. But no more than three paces, we don't want you to fall off the dais.'

In the event the king did talk to me, and very nicely. There was no trace of his stammer.

Back at the college there were just a few weeks left of my course. I saw little of Gladys before my final interview with Captain Pelly, CBE, RN, *King Alfred*'s commander. He was a great man and took real care of his cadets. I passed and was made a sub-lieutenant. I was very proud of my new uniform, made by Hope Brothers in Brighton. Of course we had a party, but there was barely time to kiss Gladys goodbye before I was given a railway warrant with immediate instructions to join HMS *Wastwater*, a converted Norwegian whaler. I groaned – another fishing boat.

5

Wastwater – the grim reality of war in the North Atlantic

The day after receiving my joining instructions, I headed north to join HMS *Wastwater*. I was told my new ship was under independent command and nobody could tell me exactly where she was. I was directed to Harwich but then told she was in Lowestoft. In the following two days she was variously reported to be in Scapa Flow, Iceland, Loch Alsh and on her way to Murmansk. Whatever else, I thought, *Wastwater* gets around.

It wasn't until the third day that I had any real intelligence.

'*Wastwater* is in Stornaway.'

'Is that definite?' I asked.

'Yes,' replied a harassed officer, slamming the phone down. I didn't dare ask the officer how to get to the Outer Hebrides, some forty miles off the northwest coast of Scotland. A railway guide provided the answer: a train to Ullapool and then a ferry. It seemed straightforward but I double-checked on a large-scale map. As far as I was concerned, the Outer Hebrides might as well have been Timbuktu.

Finally, four days after starting off from Brighton I arrived at Ullapool. It wasn't much of a town but, to my relief, there was a ferry alongside – battered, dingy, uncomfortable, but sound and serviceable, its next and only stop Stornoway. When we arrived at the port the ferry anchored offshore. I wondered what was happening. Perhaps the port would send a tender. But no, Stornoway, it transpired, was a highly religious place in those days.

Everyone, but everyone, observed the Sabbath so there was no one to tend to the ferry's lines. Another uncomfortable night. You try sleeping on wooden slats. Be they in a train or a ferry, the result is the same, aching muscles and no real sleep.

At dawn I stamped around the ferry's deck. It was a calm and sunny morning and I could not help but appreciate the beauty and safety of that marvellous harbour. Alongside was a naval trawler. Was that my new ship?

It wasn't, but the captain, an engaging and friendly man, told me he was bound for Reykjavik, where I would be sure to find the *Wastwater* sooner or later – 'unless she's sunk,' he added. 'Come on board and be my guest.'

Stornoway to Reykjavik is about two days' steaming. I remember little of the voyage except for a comfortable and welcoming bunk.

It was Wednesday when we reached Reykjavik and I finally reported on board my new ship. She looked alright, a sturdy Norwegian whaler with a Victorian gun on the forecastle and a row of depth charges on her stern. But the ship's most potent weapon was its sonar, able to detect enemy submarines below the surface of the sea. The ship's paint was peeling and there were rust patches and numerous dents and scratches on the topsides, but that's how all our ships looked in the North Atlantic, except perhaps for the destroyers, which somehow managed to retain something of their swagger.

I walked up the gangway. There was a lieutenant on the forecastle, tall, dark-haired well dressed, who I took to be the captain.

I drew myself to attention and saluted. 'Sub-Lieutenant Jones reporting for duty and training, sir.'

I was barely acknowledged, but I could smell something – aftershave? 'Follow me, please,' said the captain, and he took me below the forecastle to the seamen's mess.

I was horrified. In the mess were seventeen American sailors, all in a pitiful condition, some barely conscious, with their lower limbs frostbitten, white and deathly cold.

'We picked up these men off Greenland on our last patrol,'

explained the captain. 'They had been in a waterlogged boat for some ten days and are lucky to be alive. What are we to do?'

. 'Have you washed their limbs with fresh water?' I asked. 'That'll get the salt out.'

'Of course,' snarled the captain. 'And now we're out of fresh water.'

Again I tried to explain why I was on board but the captain didn't seem to notice. Luckily there was a shout from the deck – 'Medical officer on board, sir.'

'And who the hell are you then?' demanded the captain, turning to me.

'I've come aboard for training, sir,' I repeated.

'Then get out of my sight.'

What a welcome! To this day I cannot get those poor sailors out of my mind. All but one had to have their legs amputated. I never saw their captain; he had been locked in one of our cabins; he had lost his mind.

Despite the horror of my arrival, I soon realised that the *Wastwater* was an efficient and well-run ship. The first lieutenant was a charming and pleasant man, fair-haired, something of an academic, very thin and quiet but efficient and conscientious. He was a very different kind of man from our captain. Lieutenant Jackson RNR, the captain, was a heavy drinker who had grown to hate his first lieutenant. I never knew why, but it was a situation that was to grow more serious.

A few days later we sailed from Reykjavik for the North Cape. Our instructions, to escort two American freighters bound for Murmansk with supplies for Russia. To my great surprise the captain asked me to take the ship to sea, an unusual instruction for a newly promoted sub-lieutenant.

'Of course, sir! Let go forard! Slow astern! Stop engine! Let go spring! Let go aft! Slow ahead.'

Soon we were at sea and on our way, mercifully without a scratch. I was very proud of myself. *Wastwater*, with a single prop, was not an easy ship to handle.

The cabin I had been allocated was just above the steering motor, very noisy and in any weather extremely uncomfortable, so it was almost impossible to sleep. The real problem, however, was that to get from my cabin to the bridge in any kind of a sea meant clambering over the main engine casing. Sometimes there were lifelines, sometimes there weren't. From the second day I slept in the wardroom. But on the bridge there was little or no comfort. Cold, windy and pitching into a heavy sea, we were sodden in minutes.[7]

For the most part our voyage to the North Cape was uneventful. The two American freighters were little more than tramp steamers and made heavy weather in the North Atlantic swell. One rolled so violently that I wondered whether she would make it. Our *Wastwater*, although very small, was an excellent sea boat built by the Norwegians for the North Atlantic's troubled waters. My duty as a watch keeping officer was to take the middle and afternoon watch, and I settled into the routine. In addition I helped with the navigation and assisted our lone signalman. Throughout our escort duty our three-man Asdic team searched the ocean beneath us for any sign of the enemy. 'Ping,' went our transmitter, and subconsciously we listened for a reply. There was no contact on that voyage, except for the occasional reflected wave from a shoal of fish or, once, a whale. On the fifth night we had a remarkable display of the northern lights, aurora borealis, coloured bands of light from horizon to horizon, and sometimes dancing green men, mysterious and dramatic.

We were less than a hundred miles from the North Cape when we were relieved by a Russian destroyer who would escort our American charges to Murmansk or Archangel. Job done, we turned for home, course west-south-west, eleven knots. The first two days of our voyage to Reykjavik were quiet and uneventful, but on the third day the glass began to drop, slowly at first, and then like a stone. We were in for a blow.

By 1900 it was blowing forty knots and gusting fifty-five, a full gale but nothing unusual for the North Atlantic, even in April. The wind backed to southerly. At 2000 I turned in to try and get some sleep before my middle watch. I slept in my clothes and my oilskins – it

---

[7] In the 1940s most ships' bridges were open to the elements.

was next to impossible to dress in a small cabin pitching and rolling forty degrees or more. I could hear the wind rising and was aware that the *Wastwater* had reduced speed and altered course to head into the wind. For a while things were quieter but once again the wind began to shriek and the ship juddered, hitting one wave and another and another. Then, a crash from the stern and it seemed that the *Wastwater* might keel over. The alarm bell sounded. Something serious had happened.

It was a scene from hell. Our mast was down and pieces were scattered everywhere together with a tangle of wires, but, much more dangerous, two depth charges had broken loose and were careering up and down and across the deck. When a wave broke on *Wastwater*'s bows the water could be waist deep on the main deck and it took all my strength to remain upright. It was impossible to speak or hear, but our crew knew what to do. Of course most of them had been fishermen and had faced such danger before, but to me it was miraculous that within an hour our depth charges, the tangle of wires and the bits of broken mast had all been secured or thrown over the side. 'She will not look a pretty sight when we see her in the morning,' said Leading Seaman John Morrison, our coxswain.

I was cold and my teeth were chattering when finally I began my watch. Every bone in my body ached. But despite the great waves still breaking over our bows we sensed the worst was over. The crew on watch were remarkably cheerful. Well, after all, we had survived the tempest and nobody had been lost. A mug of cocoa and some wet sandwiches had never tasted so good. How strong was the blow? The ship's instruments had been broken so we couldn't be sure. The coxswain reckoned one-hundred-mile-an-hour gusts, others more. But all agreed that the real damage was done when the cold front passed through and the wind suddenly changed its direction.

Three days later we were back in Reykjavik. Once again the captain asked me to take over. It was a difficult approach to our berth and I took my time. I had to ring for full astern when we were in danger of being blown onto the harbour jetty. The captain grunted as we secured. I had no idea whether or not he had approved of my performance. I was happy with my new ship and our crew but I had a sense of unease about the captain. His inexplicable loathing of the first lieutenant made all of us uncomfortable.

6

Iceland, 1941

I must tell you about Iceland. My first impression was hardly favourable. Reykjavik was yet another port, cold and damp with an all-pervading smell of fish. Most of the streets were unpaved, there were no trains or trams, and the place seemed an improbable blend of frontier town and capital. Yet strangely, with a population of only some fifteen thousand, there was an abundance of bookshops carrying almost as many English and German as Icelandic publications. Before the war Germany had invested heavily in Iceland, and I wondered whether Icelanders might have preferred a German invasion to a British one.

The Icelandic people treasured their independence but, following the German invasion of Denmark in 1940, British armed forces seized their country. If the Battle of the Atlantic was to be won then a base in Iceland was essential for our ships, and in particular for the Russian convoys. Our relations with the Icelandic people were difficult, and no wonder; the invasion had happened with no warning. It was a 'them and us' situation. We were tolerated rather than welcomed. Still, there were some surprises. Many of the girls, wearing silk stockings and hats made in England, were gorgeous.

One consequence of this bad feeling was that we had great trouble getting a new mast. There were plenty of riggers in the port who could have helped but no one was prepared to do so. Eventually a small factory on the harbour front agreed to do the work, but the proprietor didn't want to break ranks, at least not publicly.

'We'll make your mast and put it outside our factory when we go home this evening, but you must collect it and do the rest of the work.'

Our first lieutenant agreed – he had no choice, we needed a mast. So a party from our ship collected the mast after dark and carried it to the *Wastwater*. Within two days our seamen had the mast up and everything in good order.

In Reykjavik itself the locals were polite but, as in the dockyard, distant and anxious lest they appeared too friendly. Ask a girl for a dance at the Borg, the town's premier dance hall (many of them were so very pretty) and she would get to her feet, but wouldn't talk. I couldn't put up with that. The only man on our ship to get up home, as it was delicately put, was the captain. I was right – he did wear aftershave, lots of it.

Iceland itself was a much larger island than I'd imagined. It is a harsh country with few inhabitants outside Reykjavik. There are no trees, only a volcanic and mountainous interior, both wild and rocky. Of course it has its geysers and hot pools, but it's not a place where I would wish to live. On our free days, and there weren't many of them, we tried to make the best of it. We even went on a skiing expedition using German skis captured in the Norwegian campaign. For Allied shipping, Iceland became a haven with its port, its fjords and sheltered anchorages, which, thanks to the Gulf Stream, were ice-free.

In the overall scheme of things *Wastwater* was a very small ship, and as a consequence we were given all kinds of odd jobs that nobody else wanted to do – collecting and delivering troops and provisions from one part of the island to another, looking for survivors, escorting stragglers, and once acting as a liberty boat. So, while we operated from Reykjavik, we were rarely in harbour for more than a few days. For the first month or two I never saw the enemy, and our voyages were uneventful. Our first lieutenant had the answer: 'Geoffrey, we're too small to bother with. They're after bigger fish than us.'

But on our next return from Cape Farewell we met a different enemy. Just one day's steaming short of Akureyri, off the northern tip of Iceland, a stiff wind was blowing from the north; it was a clear starlit night, and bitterly cold. Slowly at first, the ship began to ice. Icing is always dangerous but especially for small ships, and at the time the *Wastwater* was short of fuel and high in the water. If left, the ice would make our ship unstable and subject to capsize. The order was given, 'All hands on deck!' Armed with hammers, chisels and a steam-pipe we set to work, chipping at the ice which grew at an alarming rate – spray froze as soon as it hit our topsides. There was much grumbling – 'I'm just off watch. Why can't the fucking seamen do it, I'm a stoker' – but it was a job that had to be done for all our sakes.[8]

On returning to Reykjavik, the captain, as usual, told me to bring our ship alongside. If only something could be done about our captain's relations with his first lieutenant. I was becoming a go-between and I didn't like it, not one bit.

On 18 May we were given instructions to return to the Cape, this time independently. Our task was to search for survivors seen off the southern tip of Greenland. It was not a job that any of us enjoyed. In those cold waters our searches were rarely successful. It was an unpleasant job hoisting dead bodies on board, and on the rare occasions when we found survivors their condition could be terrible beyond belief.

At 0800 we sailed from Reykjavik. Later we passed the entrance of Hvalfjörður, where we saw HMS *Hood* at anchor. On a grey morning, she was a magnificent sight. For years she had been the most celebrated ship in the Royal Navy. A 42,100-ton battle cruiser, the world's largest and most famous warship, with her long, low hull and finely balanced silhouette she had become the embodiment of British sea power. The *Hood* had been the flagship at the Battle of Mers-el-Kébir in 1940, when the British, afraid that the French navy would fall into German hands, had destroyed many of its ships. Usually she was stationed in Scapa Flow. 'I wonder what she is doing here,' mused our coxswain as the great ship disappeared from view behind the rocky cliffs which

---

[8] Icing in the stormy north Atlantic waters was and still is extremely dangerous. The next year, on 9 March 1942, Armed Whaler HMS *Shera* was capsized by severe icing on the upper deck.

marked the entrance of the fjord.

As we passed the *Hood* the skies cleared, and for the rest of our voyage the weather was exceptional, calm with unbroken sunshine from dawn to dusk. Several miles off Greenland we could hear the grumble and see the splash of great lumps of ice falling into the ocean from the glaciers on the coast. The largest pieces would become icebergs, ice-blue mountains on a blue-green sea. After three days of searching and finding nothing we turned for home.

Nearing Reykjavik, we received a signal. 'Immediately on arrival, captain and navigating officer are to report to Command without delay, together with charts and log.'

We wondered at the order. At Command, the base navigating officer examined our log and our positions minutely.

'You were there,' he said, 'you must have heard something.'

'What do you mean?' our captain asked.

'I calculate you were within fifteen miles of the sinking of the *Hood*.'

We were horrified. 'We never saw a thing,' we told the officer.

'But you must have heard the explosion and gunfire.'

I was really upset. I loved our great British warships, and found the news unbelievable.

The so-called Battle of Denmark Strait between the *Bismarck*, the *Hood*, and the new British battleship the *Prince of Wales*, which I had seen launched in Birkenhead, had ended in disaster. It was an event that shocked the Royal Navy, the nation and the world. The *Hood*, we heard, had opened fire on *Bismarck* and the German cruiser *Prinz Eugen* as they steamed through the Denmark Strait. Early in battle the *Hood* was hit amidships by the *Bismarck*. It took just four salvos before the *Hood* exploded in flames and clouds of black smoke. Her bow rose above the water and she was gone.

The *Prince of Wales*, also seriously damaged, managed to strike the *Bismarck*'s bow compartments, leaving the battleship listing to port, leaking oil and losing speed. The battle lasted a mere seventeen minutes from opening shot to ceasefire.

The *Bismarck*, weighing over 50,000 tons, was the most powerful battleship that had ever been launched. Despite being shadowed by the British cruisers *Suffolk* and *Norfolk*, her escape towards occupied France was only foiled by brave men from the *Ark Royal* flying outdated Fairey Swordfish planes with open cockpits. After several attempts a Swordfish managed to torpedo the German ship's steering gear, further disabling her. The subsequent delay in *Bismarck*'s progress afforded enough time for a British battle fleet, Force H, to circle and then sink her less than two hundred miles from the French coast. The great warship went down fighting to the last.

We grieved for the *Hood*. There were just three survivors, together with another three sailors who had been locked up ashore for misdemeanours. One occasion, I guess, when crime paid.

7

Spitsbergen, summer 1941

If there was a best time to be at sea in the North Atlantic it was surely the summer months, when the weather, for some of the time, could be tolerable, although even then there would be days of gales, heavy rain and sudden squalls of sleet and snow. But the most worrying times for our convoys and their crews were the quiet, sunlit days when it would be easy for our enemies to find us. Smoke from our ships, particularly from the coal burners, would hang in the air and German reconnaissance planes would appear, circling slowly just out of range. Then, as often as not, U-boats would make an appearance. By the spring of 1941 most of the U-boats in the North Atlantic were hunting in packs. And so it was that during a long summer's day our sailors would pray for typical North Atlantic weather: cloud, rain, snow, sleet, fog or, failing that, a gale.

Allied shipping losses in 1941 were unsustainable, but our navy was at last making headway in dealing with the U-boat menace. Our ships were better equipped and our men better trained in detecting and destroying our underwater enemies. Then on 22 June came the news that Germany had invaded Russia. 'The silly bastards, they're done for,' was the reaction of some our ship's company, but I wasn't so sure.

The invasion altered the whole balance of power in Europe, and Churchill seized the opportunity. Russia could be a formidable ally against the Nazis. It was agreed that our navy would keep the shipping lanes open to Murmansk and Archangel. Easier said than done, but the commitment was made.

Within a month the newly promoted Rear Admiral Philip Vian

was tasked with setting up an advance naval base on the island of Spitsbergen, five hundred miles north of Norway. Despite the distance it was felt that that the island could hold the key to protecting the passage to Russia's northern ports. Admiral Vian had distinguished himself in the battle to sink the *Bismarck*, and in July he sailed from Reykjavik for Spitsbergen with two cruisers and two destroyers. Anchored off Reykjavik we saw Vian's ships sail, but had no idea of what was afoot. We were soon to find out. Just a day later we received orders to escort a fleet tanker, our destination – Spitsbergen.

Heading north there was no ice, no contact with the enemy, and our mission was accomplished without incident. But, in Spitsbergen we found a hive of activity. Among the assembled ships was none other than the *Adventure*, my last ship. Why on earth had she been brought to this desolate place? She was after all a minelayer. It was strange to meet up with some of my old comrades, and despite my now being a 'fucking officer' I was made very welcome. To my great delight Electrical Officer James was also on board. I was glad to see a friend; it was August bank holiday and I was far from home.

Our next assignment was to escort SS *Dagney*, an old collier with sixty-seven Norwegian passengers and crew, back to the UK. All went well until the last stage of our journey when we were bombed near the Faroes. There was nothing we could do to protect ourselves. Our Victorian gun with a maximum elevation of forty-five degrees was useless and the bomber plane, a Dornier, kept clear of our small arms. *Dagney* was sunk. She wasn't hit, but a couple of near misses were sufficient to open the old ship's plates and she filled with water. Happily we were able to get alongside before she sank and there were no serious casualties. Nonetheless quite a few of our Norwegian friends needed medical attention. Our cook, who had been trained in first aid, was quick and efficient. I too had some first aid training so I set about giving the cook a hand – he dealing with three patients to my one. There was one Norwegian who I thought had broken his leg; he was groaning and in obvious pain. So, taking some trouble, I improvised a splint, and was pleased with my handiwork. The following morning we put him ashore in Torshavn, the largest town in the Faroes, where there was an army garrison. Later that day we received a signal from the garrison doctor: 'The medical care you gave to the Norwegians was excellent, with one exception. You put a splint of sorts on a man's leg. I have no idea why – the leg was not broken, it was deformed.'

The bombing had made it crystal clear that while we might keep a submarine at bay we were a sitting duck for enemy aircraft. Yet again our first lieutenant made an indent for a new gun. Our old Victorian firing piece might look handsome, but in the Battle of the Atlantic she was a liability. I was more afraid of her than of the enemy. As gunnery officer for *Wastwater* I have to say I hated the bloody thing. And there was another problem. I noticed, and not before time, that the rating in charge of our guns was an awful shot. On investigation we found he had astigmatism. The cook volunteered to stand in. 'I used to do some shooting,' he explained. We found him excellent, and from then on when there was a call to action stations he would man the guns and our previous gunner would make the sandwiches.

Meanwhile the Spitsbergen saga was still going on. Although the admiral had been made welcome by all the inhabitants (with the exception of three German radio operators who had been stationed there), Vian was convinced that this frozen Norwegian island was overexposed to enemy attack, and that the winter ice would make it an unsatisfactory naval base. The Admiralty and indeed Churchill himself accepted Vian's report, and he was ordered back to the island with instructions to destroy its mining facilities and fuel stocks, repatriate the Russians, and bring the Norwegians and any available ships back to Britain. The only ship that was lost throughout the entire operation was the poor old *Dagney*.

This all sounds straightforward, but the distances that Admiral Vian and his ships travelled on this campaign were over seven thousand miles, which gives some idea of the scale and size of the North Atlantic waters.

The following day we left the Faroes for Scapa – back to my old hunting ground. I was becoming fond of the place.

8

We lose our captain but find a submarine

When we arrived in Scapa Flow we were instructed to secure to a buoy off the small harbour of Lyness on the island of Hoy. The port was nothing more than a fishing village, with limited space alongside. True to form, as soon as we had secured our captain, a bottle of whisky under his arm, was off to see a friend of his in the base ship, *Dunlow Castle*. Later that evening he returned – drunk, but no worse than usual, and none of us were concerned. For myself I was pleased that we were not alongside – with luck I would get an undisturbed night's sleep, and our crew needed a rest. The voyage from Spitsbergen had taken an age, and we were sorry that the *Dagney* had been sunk.

I was sitting alone in the wardroom which often doubled as my cabin when a worried-looking John Morrison, the coxswain, knocked on the door.

'We have a problem, sir. The captain has a gun and says he is determined to shoot the first lieutenant.'

'Why, in heaven's name? And how the hell did he get a gun?'

'I gave it to him. He made a request. As captain he's entitled.'

'What about ammunition?'

'He's got plenty of rounds in his bedside locker.'

'Where's the first lieutenant?'

'I think he's asleep.'

'What about the captain?'

'He's in his cabin, or was a moment ago.'

'We'd better go and see.'

We stood together in a small lobby outside the captain's cabin.

There was shouting, swearing, the sound of objects being hurled round the room. 'I will get you, you fucking bastard, I've got a gun and I'm going to use it.' He sounded delirious and dangerous. I had simply no idea what I should do.

And then it came to me – what would any officer do in such circumstances? He would send a signal. That is exactly what I did, and here it is, word for word:

TO   ADMIRAL COMMANDING ORKNEY AND SHETLAND

FROM   SUB LIEUTENANT JONES HMS WASTWATER

       CAPTAIN IS THREATENING TO SHOOT FIRST

       LIEUTENANT REQUEST INSTRUCTIONS

I never did get a reply. We kept watch outside the cabin and maybe an hour later the noise began to subside. Nervously we opened the door, the coxswain taking the lead. As he heard the door click the captain opened his eyes and fixed them on me; he was furious. I hastily withdrew and hid myself behind the door while the coxswain, who had always got on rather well with the captain, tried gently to talk him down. A little later I eased the door open again and saw the gun lying on a side-table. I leant over the coxswain and picked it up. The crisis was over.

A few minutes later a launch from Command came alongside, and a large warrant officer and four seamen came on board. It was obvious that this officer too had been drinking, probably Scotch, the standard drink in Scapa.

'Is your captain still armed?' demanded the warrant officer, sweating and nervous.

'No,' I told him, 'we've got his gun.'

'Thank God for that!' He was visibly relieved.

Five minutes later the captain was in the launch. One of the seamen had put his cap on his head and his coat round his shoulders. I remember it was a very cold night.

'That's the last we will see of him,' said Morrison.

I, however, was not so lucky.

The first lieutenant had slept through the entire proceedings. He merely shrugged his shoulders when we told him that the captain had been arrested. On board there had been a rumour that

Jackson had started life as an east coast fisherman and had joined the merchant navy as a senior steward. Somehow, the rumour went, on the outbreak of war he had managed to convince the authorities that he had been captain of a fishing boat and as such was appointed an RNR lieutenant. Was that the cause of the trouble? Did the first lieutenant know of Jackson's subterfuge? Or was the captain jealous of the first lieutenant, an assured and well-educated man?

In a way I was sorry for Jackson. He had never shirked his duty and had never done me any harm. Far from that, Jackson had trusted me, given me the opportunity to make decisions and take the lead. Under his command I had grown up. Perhaps the rumour was nothing but a rumour, and the simple truth was that a year as a captain in the North Atlantic had been too much for him. A number of other officers had cracked under the unrelenting pressure and responsibility.

Some six weeks later I was called as a witness to the captain's court martial, a miserable experience when Jackson was dismissed his ship. Before the court martial Jackson had made things much worse for himself. Released from hospital, he had asked a paymaster for an advance. On being refused, he had punched the unfortunate man and knocked him to the ground. Not once, while I was in court, did Jackson look in my direction, nor did he in my hearing offer so much as a word in his own defence.

Strangely enough, the ship's company took little notice of the crisis. Thinking about it, I suppose none of us had the time to worry. We were too busy coping with our own jobs and wondering whether we would survive our next convoy. Our seamen in particular were philosophical. Life had always been hard for them – fishing is a rough, tough and dangerous business. Half our seamen came from Grimsby, the rest from the Hebrides, including our coxswain, who claimed to be descended from the survivors of the Spanish Armada. They got on well and were excellent hands. The Stornoway men, despite their strict religious upbringing, were always laughing and joking. Much merriment was caused by having two Jim McClouds in the crew –

'Jim, you're late for your watch.'

'It's not this Jim, sir, it's the other Jim.'

There were about thirty of us in total. We had five engine-room staff, an electrician, four officers, a signalman, four men for the depth charges and the guns, three for the Asdics, a cook, and a steward. All in all *Wastwater* was a happy ship, blessed with a sense of comradeship and gallows humour. Nevertheless, every ship has its skate and we had ours. One day I lost my wallet. By then I had learnt a thing or two about taking care of myself and I knew where it had gone.

As I passed the culprit on the upper deck I tapped his shoulder. 'If I don't get that wallet back, you're going for a swim. Do I make myself clear?' I hissed.

'Yes sir,' was the mumbled reply.

My wallet was duly returned. A skate maybe, but our thief was a good seaman and a popular man with a sense of humour. For several months he behaved himself, and then he jumped ship. I've no idea what happened to him.

The day after our captain's departure, *Dunlow Castle* sent a launch to collect me. I was instructed to report to a Captain Down and bring *Wastwater*'s wine and spirit book with me. Captain Down was an officer of the old school, a four-ring Royal Naval captain who wore a cloth over his sleeves to keep his gold braid sparkling. He listened to my story.

'You've done well,' he said. 'Now, how much does the captain owe the wardroom for his wine and spirit?'

'Fifteen pounds, sir.'

'I'll see you get it right away. I don't want any of my officers in debt.'

Before I left a paymaster handed me the fifteen pounds.

Then our new captain, Lieutenant John May, came on board. He was a pipe-smoking, mild-mannered Londoner whose father was the writer and Catholic convert, J Lewis May. He had already been awarded the OBE, and had spent six years in the merchant navy. A few days later we were again on escort duty.

On leaving Scapa our new captain gave me both an instruction and a compliment. 'I want you to carry on, Sub, and drive the ship. I hear you're better at handling these tubs than most of us.'

I was delighted, and I sensed, as did the crew, that he was the right man for *Wastwater*.

On our way back to Reykjavik we received a signal, 'A U-boat has been surfaced and surrendered to one of our aircraft.'

As I put the position of the captured submarine on our chart I gasped. It was unbelievable. The submarine was within half a day's sail. 'Full speed ahead!' It was an order rarely given. Would we get there in time?

We didn't learn all that had happened until much later, but here is the story of how the incident unfolded. On 27 August 1941, Squadron Leader J Thompson of Coastal Command spotted U-Boat U-570 proceeding on the surface. The submarine had been at sea barely seventy-two hours and was on her maiden operational voyage. Thompson swooped and dropped four depth charges set to explode at minimum depth, causing enough damage for the crew to appear in lifejackets on the submarine's conning tower. Thompson made his second pass at one hundred feet, raking the sub with his machine gun and threatening unrelenting fire on the crew if there were any attempt to scuttle. There was an exchange of light signals, swiftly followed by the German captain running up a white flag and indicating that all he wanted was for his crew to be rescued. Thompson continued to circle overhead until relieved a little later by a Catalina.

We ourselves reached the submarine the following morning. The U-boat was stationary, rolling in a moderate sea with our sister ship, the *Kingston Agate*, close by. Suddenly proceedings were enlivened by an American four-stack destroyer which appeared out of nowhere and fired over our heads. We were aghast at the intervention and nervous, there was every chance she would hit us or the submarine. But in the end all was well. We assured the American destroyer that we had the matter in hand and she sailed on her way.

Our first and most difficult task was to get the submarine in tow – much easier said than done. I manoeuvred the *Wastwater* upwind of the U-boat and the crew enjoyed hurling lines at our stricken enemy. But that was no good, we were unable to persuade any of the German crew to come down from their conning tower. So it was left to Jock Campbell, the first lieutenant of the *Kingston Agate*, and a leading hand to secure a tow. The two of them took a line by Carley float to the submarine and, after a struggle, made it fast. It was a hazardous undertaking – the sea wasn't particularly rough, but it wasn't calm either. No sooner had the *Kingston Agate* begun the tow than she was assigned to another job and *Windermere*, another armed trawler which had arrived later in the forenoon, took over. The *Wastwater* was ordered to escort this unusual procession towards Iceland. Twenty-four hours later we grounded the submarine on one of the island's few beaches.

A team of skilled artificers inspected the ship. The artificers found little damage, and the only explanation for the submarine's capture seemed to be a remarkable lack of will on the part of the German captain and his crew. Six months later the U-570 was commissioned in the Royal Navy and renamed HMS *Graph*. For the rest of the war she flew the white ensign. I learnt later that soon after capture, Rahmlow, the U-boat commander, committed suicide.

Once alongside in Reykjavik it appeared that everybody wanted to talk to us. We enjoyed all the attention enormously. It was quite a change from being the Cinderella of the fleet. And there was another surprise. The Yanks had arrived, and in huge numbers – they were everywhere. The United States had taken over responsibility for Iceland. Equipment, stores, guns, trucks littered the port, which now seemed to be under the control of a remarkable man, Captain Rivers of the First Stevedoring Company of America. A real boss man, he enjoyed marching up and down the Town Quay giving orders to everyone. He was also hugely sociable, and in between times he was only too happy to be invited on board for a drink.

One day a large armoured truck was being hoisted into the air from a freighter when a wire strap broke and the vehicle went straight through the dockyard piles, making a large hole.

'What are you going to do about that, Captain Rivers?' I asked. 'It's going to be difficult to get the vehicle out.'

'Get the vehicle out? Hell no,' replied the stevedore, 'we won't even try. We'll just board it over.' And that is exactly what they did.

From that moment I was sure that with America's help we would win the war.

Just a few miles north of Reykjavik, Hvalfjörður was full of ships. American, British and Allied forces were everywhere, with new army and navy encampments all along the shore. Hvalfjörður is one of the most extraordinary fjords in the world. A naturally secure harbour, during the war it was used as an anchorage and refuelling base. The entry to the fjord was spectacular. It was lined on either side by granite mountains of two thousand feet or more, the tops covered with a sprinkling of snow. Here and there on the lower slopes were settlements, hamlets looking as if they had been painted on the gloomy backdrop of the hills. There were no trees. The locals, men, women and children, had red cheeks and were for all practical purposes self-sufficient. They survived on long-coated sheep, ducks, fish from the fjord, and occasionally horse meat from the ponies that pulled their two-wheeled carts. It was a desperately hard life, played out in weather that could turn a man mad.

While *Wastwater* had been engaged in the Spitsbergen affair, Winston Churchill had met with President Roosevelt in Placentia Bay, Newfoundland. He had been taken across the Atlantic on the battleship *Prince of Wales*, for much of the time unguarded, as the escort ships had been unable to keep station in the heavy weather. As a result of the meeting an Atlantic Charter had been agreed: henceforth Atlantic convoys would have American escorts to Cape Farewell.[9] This may not have meant much to the British public, but it was great news for us and the British fleet. On his safe return to Reykjavik, with President Roosevelt's son standing at his side, Churchill addressed many of the Icelanders from the president's palace. Always the orator, his speech was a great success, and he was cheered to the echo. The Icelanders liked a fighter; good

---

[9] Churchill and Roosevelt met for the first time in Placentia Bay, Newfoundland, between 8 and 11 August 1941. The outcome was the creation of the Atlantic Charter, an agreement between Britain and America that led to an Anglo-American alliance. Churchill arrived in some style, and much enjoyed his voyage on Britain's newest battleship.

relations were restored.

For the next few weeks it was back to our normal routine. We never knew what our next orders would bring, but we knew that autumn was approaching. The weather would get worse and we would have to cope with hour upon hour of darkness. It was a prospect that filled me with some dread. On several occasions we joined the big convoys, usually at Cape Farewell. A forty-ship convoy with its escorts is a remarkable sight. We were normally stationed at the very rear or the very wing of the escorts. Chivvying up a straggler or filling a gap in the screen was a regular duty. On one trip from Cape Farewell we spent most of our time looking after an elderly Greek freighter. The weather was good and the freighter, a coal burner, was making too much smoke.

'Tell the Greek to stop making smoke,' was the commodore's instruction.

We went alongside and shouted at the Greek captain. Had he understood? He nodded, and the smoke subsided.

Four hours later, another signal. 'Tell the Greek freighter to resume his station.'

The Greek put his thumbs in the air and once again clouds of black smoke issued from the old freighter's funnel. Perhaps it was not a coincidence when later we were instructed to detach from the convoy and escort three ships to Liverpool, one of those the Greek. All went well and we were pleased to get out of the North Atlantic for a while. You might think that following our success we would have been rewarded with a few hours ashore in my home town, but things didn't work like that. The moment the ships were delivered, it was back to Scapa. Or was it back to Reykjavik? To be honest, I can't remember. It was a long time ago.

In early autumn we had a new first lieutenant, one Michael Thwaites, a talented man, an Australian, an Empire loyalist, a writer, a poet and a member of the Oxford Movement. He became a great friend. Sometimes at night I could hear him talking.

One day I challenged him – 'Who are you talking to?'

'To God,' was the reply.

After Michael's arrival more of our work concentrated on delivering single ships or small groups to UK ports. It was fortunate for us that the shallow seas round England were dangerous for U-boats. Bombs and mines were the greater threat. Still, we didn't lose a single ship and were justly proud of our record.

9

Aberdeen, then back to the frozen north

There were just the three of us – Michael Thwaites, the most conscientious of first lieutenants, John May and myself. I could hardly think of a more agreeable wardroom. As for the ship's company, as Michael soon found, they were a crowd of cheerful, bloody-minded individualists. There was no doubt but that our crew would come together, fight the enemy and deal with any emergency with spirit and courage, but Michael, like most first lieutenants, wanted that bit more. I kept in the background but was greatly amused watching Michael's daily tussle with Leading Seaman John Morrison, our coxswain.

'I want to get on with painting the deck today, Morrison.'

'Aye aye sir, but it's not a good day for painting.'

'Why not?'

'We've only got that dark grey in the store. It's not the right shade. Besides, there's rain coming. I think I'll get on with that splicing job'.

Morrison was an artist when it came to splicing of any kind, including wire. Nevertheless, *Wastwater* was soon the smartest ship in the squadron.

Meanwhile we looked forward to the boiler clean, which would allow all of us some leave. At last we had orders to sail independently for Aberdeen, where the dockyard had space for us. As soon as *Wastwater* docked I caught the train for London and, to my surprise and despite the devastation caused by the Luftwaffe, we arrived at Euston bang on time.

It was so very good to see Gladys. On our first evening together, we decided to marry.

'I'll make the arrangements for your next leave,' she said.

'That should be in May,' I told her.

She sighed and kissed me. A spring wedding! If I get through the bloody winter, I thought, remembering the cold rough seas, the dark and the screech of enemy bombers.

All too quickly leave was over, and just seven days later I was back in Aberdeen. In my absence there had been some serious German air raids on the Granite City and a bomb had destroyed a merchantman close to *Wastwater*. There had been an explosion and a tremendous fire. 'It was impossible to look at the ship,' one of the dockyard workers told me, 'the flames were so hot.' Miraculously most of the ship's crew had survived. I had learnt by then how unpredictable explosions can be. A seaman standing close to where the mine had all but destroyed the *Adventure* had survived unscathed while others on the bridge had been severely wounded.

Before the end of November we were back in Iceland. The weather in the winter months of 1941 and 1942 was worse than anything the locals could remember, the winds varying from flat calm, gale to hurricane in just an hour or two and the cycle endlessly repeating itself. We soon had our orders. We were to escort a small convoy round the west coast of Iceland and deliver the ships some three hundred miles north of Iceland where Allied escorts would take over. In pitch darkness and high, short seas navigation round the rocky headlands of the west coast was not easy. Keeping our ships together was another problem. Was that shadow to starboard a cliff or the elderly merchantman, part of our convoy which we hadn't seen in the last eight hours? Convoy work at the best of times was a dangerous business, and in the winter months there would only be a short period of daylight, 1000 to 1500, five precious hours.

Eventually, on the fourth day at sea, we made contact with the Allied convoy. Our four ships joined their sixteen ships. We watched anxiously as the ships, including the elderly merchantman which had rejoined us a day later, altered course for the east, the North Cape and Russia. I tried to say a prayer for them but soon hurried below for the warmth of the wardroom. *Wastwater* altered course, south for Akureyri, Iceland's second city, where we were to refuel. With any luck we would get a decent night's sleep there. But once again the weather showed its teeth. It snowed all night, and when the sun made a rare appearance at 1100 we found our ship transformed, white and ghostlike, the rigging glistening like tinsel. All very pretty, but pretty dangerous too, as I knew from my first encounter with icing the previous spring. Everybody that could be spared was up top. With axes, crowbars and shovels we slowly removed the weight of ice and snow from our decks. Later that day we posed for photographs. We were on the Russian front!

Akureyri is situated on the north coast of Iceland near the end of the longest fjord in the island, almost forty miles long. A base for rural communities, it was and is an important fishing centre. It is surrounded by high mountains and despite the northern latitude has an unusually warm climate. Not that I noticed – whenever *Wastwater* was in the vicinity it seemed one of the coldest places on earth. But the water in the fjord was calm, and after five rough days we were able to get some sleep. It was in Akureyri that Michael talked about his first-born son, who had died, and his wife Honor. He showed me a poem he had written. I was moved. While the poem laments the death of his child it also describes the magic of entering a harbour.

Coming into the Clyde

Part of me for ever is the January morning
Coming into the Clyde in the frosty moonlight
And the land under snow and the snow under moonlight,
Fall upon fall, a soundless ecstasy.
I alone on the bridge, below me the helmsman
Whistling softly to the listening voice pipe,
And no sound else than the washing of the bow-wave
As the buoys go by like marching pylons.
I gaze from the glory of the bared universe
To the guarded secret of the winter world
Rapt, and the helmsman now is silent,
And I wait for the time to alter course.
To port left the magic scenario mountains
White above the shoulders of holy island,

And nearer, clear as a square-lined coverlet,
All the fields and hedges on the slopes of Arran.
But further and smaller, away to starboard
The plaited hills of Ayrshire gleam,
And I in thought am over them all
Away to my darling and my little son.
Beyond the moonlit hills that morning
My darling lay, and my little son;
But she in her cold bed lone and waking,
And he in the frozen ground asleep.

The voyage back home from Akureyri – did I say home, that was a slip, Reykjavik was never home – was no better than our outward voyage, and this time, as if to spite us, the wind had backed and we had to steam into the teeth of a southwesterly gale. Back in Reykjavik Roads it was still blowing. We went ashore for stores and learnt that once again there was no mail. Some idiot had redirected it back to the UK.

In the afternoon we were ordered to Hvalfjörður to top up our fuel. It was unfortunate that the fuel pipe lowered down to us from the tanker – our bridge was barely level with the tanker's main deck – had a mind of its own. Suddenly there was fuel oil on our decks and our chief engineer's uniform. After a clear-up, accompanied by much cursing, our captain had a bright idea. 'I will get permission to spend the night alongside; we will return to the Roads as soon as it is light.' A calm and peaceful night was always a bonus.

It was a little after 0100 that we were struck by a hurricane bursting on us from the granite cliffs of the fjord, parting wires and moorings, sinking boats – all this while driving sleet reduced visibility to a few yards.

The quartermaster had raised the alarm. 'Our wires, sir, they have parted fore and aft and I think we're adrift.'

Soon the tanker began to drift out of sight. Checking the chart, I shouted to the captain, 'We can't go too far this way, it's three cables to the rocks.'

On the forecastle, Morrison and the first lieutenant had let go the anchor, but it wouldn't hold despite our going half-ahead.

'She's not holding an inch!' shouted one of the Grimsby lads.

On the bridge the captain remained calm. 'Let go another shackle, hard a starboard, watch the cable!'

The cable shifted and our bow came up into the wind. We were safe, for the moment.

For the next seven hours the hurricane raged and our captain, cool and confident, kept *Wastwater* steaming at half-ahead. There was chaos everywhere – ships going aground, dragging their anchors and getting in all kinds of trouble. Suddenly, just as it was beginning to get light, the wind dropped. Some of the ships in the anchorage bore the scars of collisions, and just half a mile away a small merchantman was high and dry out of the water perched on a reef, her funnel broken and drooping over her side. Later we learnt that three other ships had been grounded and lives lost. Shore stations had suffered damage too, and all the staff at the RAF base had been ordered outside to physically hang on to their planes lest they be swept away. There had even been a signal, 'One Nissan hut airborne 0330 hours, ETA 0335.' All in all it wasn't a quiet night. Indeed, it was the noise I remember best, the screeching and howling of the wind.

On Christmas Eve we were back in Reykjavik. We had just finished our dinner in the wardroom when there was the sound of feet on the deck, a flicker from a lantern and then the chorus of 'Good King Wenceslas,' well sung and led by Coxswain Morrison.

On Christmas morning we had a short service, the captain finishing with a prayer for absent families and friends. 'Amen' said our crew in one voice. Below, the mess deck was splendid – decorations of every kind, paper chains, streamers, bells, imitation holly and lots more. For Christmas dinner the cook had excelled himself: roast chicken, roast potatoes, peas, mince pies (our cook was a great pastry maker) and to finish up a plum pudding laced with half a bottle of sherry. It was a great dinner. In accordance with naval custom we three officers were mess men for the day.

'I can see you are not used to this kind of work,' said our signalman, as for the second time I dropped a plate.

Dinner finished, glasses were filled and Marcella Whiffs lighted. Mouth organs appeared and a sing song began. Old favourites were sung with gusto, and Stoker Bird gave his rendering of 'Pennies from heaven' (amended to 'kroner' for local colour). Slowly the level of entertainment began to decline from carols to bawdy songs until our youngest seaman, a gunner, spoke out.

'Come lads, you have all the year for that. This is Christmas Day!'

And so it remained. Our first lieutenant wrote a ballad about the event, sixteen verses. Here's a flavour of it:

Christmas in Iceland

We lay in Iceland winter bound
And heard the blizzard blow,
And naught we saw on sea or shore
Except the driving snow.

Then said our captain to the cook
At anchor as we lay,
'Make us a duff with all your might;
Tomorrow's Christmas Day.'

Then said the cook, a Scotsman
'My season's Hogmanay
Yet I will make a mighty duff
To eat on Christmas Day.'

On Christmas Day it still snowed on.
No news from home had we
But we'd the cook's great Christmas Duff,
And our good company.

The wind grew wild, the snow it piled
On deck your boots would freeze on,
But in the mess deck down below
We kept the Christmas season.

Christmas over, *Wastwater* was sent out on a New Year patrol, much to the disgust of our cook. It was near a crime for 'the bloody English' not to let him celebrate Hogmanay in the proper manner. Back in harbour he decided to make amends, and taking his friend the steward ashore with him he set off grimly determined to make a night of it. An hour later the two of them were back on board and not happy – the inflexible ration in the seamen's canteen, Hogmanay or no, was one bottle of beer per man.

It was a rare day when we were alongside that we did not have company. One day we berthed next to a Grimsby trawler. In minutes our Grimmies, as we called them, were on board with enough fish to keep us going for several days. Two of their skippers came aboard too and had a drink in our wardroom. They were good company and enjoyed our Scotch, and if they wondered what on earth an unlikely bunch like us were doing in charge of the sort of vessels they had been sailing since birth, they were too polite to say so.

On a trip to Hvalfjörður to refuel, we had a request from the stores officer: would we please take twenty bags of coke to the cruiser *Cumberland*. Michael was not best pleased, but in due course we went alongside to deliver as requested. It was dusk and I doubt the officer of the watch had recognised we were an HM ship. Presently a large crane swung over us and in one swoop lifted all the coke from our deck. As we were lying comfortably alongside we requested permission to stay the night. The response was immediate – approved – and was accompanied by an invitation to visit.

Climbing aboard in the most respectable suits we could muster, we marvelled at the size and order of the ship, a heavy County class cruiser. With its great guns it was seemingly invincible, although not perhaps in the face of a North Atlantic storm – a wave had destroyed the forward gun turret of a similar cruiser. Some of our hands went to the *Cumberland*'s cinema, while our reception in the wardroom could not have been warmer. The engineer commander made a handsome apology that we should have been mistaken for a coke boat. We talked long into the evening, and all agreed that none of us had known worse weather. The commander had seen the cruiser that had lost its gun turret and paid us a great compliment –

'At the end of that last blow we lost boats, smashed up, and a lot of gear. Everybody else, destroyers and the like, had returned to harbour, except us and of course you trawlers.'

Much of our conversation that evening was about the Japanese attack on Pearl Harbor.[10]

'It must be good for us in the long run,' said John May, 'but there is a long way to go.' He was right.

On our return to Reykjavik we found our mail had finally arrived, seven sacks of it, the first for two months since leaving home. A hush came over the ship – our thoughts were with our loved ones. My news was good. Gladys still loved me and was enjoying working for the fire service; she was very much looking forward to our being married in May. My three brothers were all doing well, and even my father had sent me a friendly note. Of course not everybody's news was good, and the men from Grimsby were worried, as the town had been subject to a number of fierce bombing raids.

What would the New Year bring? We were about to find out – and my wedding plans were among the casualties.

---

[10] On 7 December 1941 the Japanese navy launched a ferocious attack on the American naval base at Pearl Harbor, Hawaii, from their aircraft carriers. Many ships were sunk, many aircraft were destroyed, and there was a heavy loss of life. Immediately there was a state of war between Japan and America. Just a day later Germany declared war on America.

10

Churchill and Roosevelt
order *Wastwater* to America

Well, it didn't happen just like that. But the outbreak of war with Germany had brought alarming shipping losses for America. In the first few weeks, Dönitz's long-distance U-boats had sunk over a hundred ships off the east coast. Though powerful, America could not sustain losses of that kind. Roosevelt and Churchill, on good terms following their meeting the previous summer, considered what should be done. Yes, it would be a good idea if America could borrow twenty-four ships from the Anti-Submarine Escort Force Trawler Squadron, as our ships were called. In truth, we had never considered ourselves a squadron but we were pleased by the description – it sounded rather grand. Usually we were seen as destroyers' poor relations.

Of course we knew nothing about these plans. But in the New Year we should have realised something was up. Without notice we were told that there would be an Inspection of *Wastwater* by the admiral in command of HMS *Balder*: 'Hands to be in working rig and normal ship's routine to carry on.' We were decidedly unenthusiastic but, come the day, our ship's company played its part, as did the admiral. He spoke to everyone and made some sensible suggestions; his inspection was brief and to the point. Even the crew, deeply suspicious of unnecessary bull, conceded they had known worse. Of course the admiral found something amiss (that was his job) when he came face to face with Bill Bowie, our third engineer, puffing on a fag in the engine room. The two of them looked at each other in

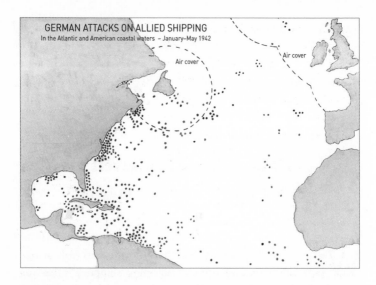

GERMAN ATTACKS ON ALLIED SHIPPING
In the Atlantic and American coastal waters – January–May 1942

Air cover

Air cover

astonishment. 'Put it out!' growled the admiral as he strode round the engine room. Back on deck he spoke to the captain. 'You have a good ship and a good ship's company,' and with that he was gone.

Two days later our captain returned to the ship following a visit to headquarters. His news came as a great surprise. Our ship, and sister ship HMS *Buttermere*, were to sail to America. The news was a blow to some of us and in particular to our first lieutenant Michael Thwaites, who had hoped against hope that he would be at home for the birth of his second child. And I was going to miss Gladys, a lot. But on reflection the news had a silver lining. None of us would miss the North Atlantic with its gales, cold, and unpredictable seas. Yes, New York in the spring had appeal. And the captain was pleased: the admiral had been told to pick his two best ships.

'At least he's right on that score,' said Michael.

In February we set sail with *Buttermere* for Halifax. It seemed that the North Atlantic wanted to make amends for the awful weather we had endured over the previous months. We had a gentle wind from the east. However, following a gale many miles away, there was a huge swell. Our ships rode comfortably as mighty waves overtook us at twice our speed, but our sterns would lift and for a moment we would be at the summit until we slid down the other side at a quickening pace. We could measure the height of the waves as in the troughs *Buttermere* all but disappeared.

For our voyage across the Atlantic *Buttermere* was the senior ship, commanded by a Lieutenant Gowther. There was an etiquette for such matters, and on leaving Reykjavik *Buttermere* was sent a signal from the senior officer: 'Being in all respects ready for war, take *Wastwater* under your arm and proceed.' And while our captain was responsible for his ship, it was *Buttermere*'s privilege to regulate our speed and course. So there we were, just the two of us alone on a vast ocean, two tiny ships, and we were to stick together. It was extraordinary, but every day the sun shone and we never saw another ship, nor any aircraft. At noon we took out our sextants and 'shot the sun', continuing a centuries-old practice. The captain, the first lieutenant and myself could never quite agree. The captain was the quickest and most skilful; his eight years in the merchant navy had given him a start. But we were all pleased and proud of our landfall just twelve miles from our dead reckoning after a voyage of some 1,400 miles. The last twelve hours had been in a thick Newfoundland fog. I was on watch and proceeding at slow ahead when I thought I heard something. Maybe it was a buoy, but there it was again and this time I was sure, it was the sound of cows mooing. I turned the ship on a reciprocal course and called the captain. We'd lost *Buttermere* in the fog a few hours previously, so we found Halifax alone. To our immense irritation, *Buttermere* was already alongside.

Secured in Halifax, the captain went ashore. It wasn't long before he returned and he was smiling. 'Orders are to proceed immediately to New York! It's fifteen years since I was in New York, Sub, you'll like it. Nip ashore and get all the latest information, charts and the like. I'll not wish to make a mess of our arrival.'

That evening we slipped. The sea was calm, and as we ploughed southward it became just a little warmer. We were excited and a little wary. We knew about the U-boats and about the ships that had been sunk by torpedo and by gun. The first lieutenant demanded a sharp lookout. Off Nantucket there was more fog, with visibility no more than a few hundred yards. 'Close to one cable' (200 yards) was the instruction from *Buttermere*, and even at that range it was difficult to keep station.

And then a shout came from one of the lookouts, 'Periscope bearing green four zero, sir!'

'Hard a starboard!' commanded the captain. 'Where?' he kept demanding, peering into the fog.

'Lost it now, sir.'

'Action stations!'

As the bells clanged we rushed to the four-inch gun – here was a real chance for us to distinguish ourselves. Astern, the depth charges were being got ready while the Asdic operator searched for a contact.

'There he is, 300 yards red two zero.'

'Fire!'

The gun's recoil rocked the ship and we saw a slim rod sticking up on our port bow. The Lewis gunners saw it too and opened fire with a deafening clatter. Then came the order from the bridge: 'Cease fire!'

The periscope passed down our side. Except it wasn't a periscope, it was just a Dan buoy laid by some local fishermen as a marker. The captain looked askance.

'Never mind, sir, we had some fun. It was a good bang, wasn't it?' said a junior member of the gun crew.

I soon had confirmation that we were getting close to New York when my homemade wireless burst into life, there was some music and then an American voice extolling the virtues of Kellogg's cornflakes. It was still foggy in Long Island Sound when we heard the dreary moan of a light ship's fog signal.

'There she is, sir,' sang out voices from those on deck. The Ambrose light vessel was soon alongside. We had arrived.

As we approached New York things began to happen. A pilot vessel drew alongside and a pilot hopped on board. 'Morning guys, I'm here to help.'

He had brought the morning paper and we were astonished at its size – pages and pages of it. As we sailed towards Staten Island he sang out the features on the shore. 'Sandy Hook, Coney Island, the outskirts of Brooklyn and the Forts.'

Then, as we neared Manhattan, the fog melted away and we were witness to one of the most extraordinary sights in all the world: the great skyscrapers, the Empire State Building, the crowded anchorages and the myriad of tugs and ferries which crisscrossed the water. I marvelled. I had never seen anything like it. Ahead of us, the piers and houses of Staten Island.

It was difficult to think of the war when we arrived in New York, so different from the bleak, inhospitable fjords of Iceland and the blacked-out ports and cities of Britain. Nevertheless, we had arrived at a time of crisis. Allied shipping losses on the east coast were now over three hundred, some being sunk by enemy U-boats, by gun and by torpedo, in full view of the shore. Ships from our squadron were moving into position all along the eastern seaboard. It was an almost seamless operation, except that one of our craft, mistaken for the enemy, was rammed by an American destroyer.

11

New York, New York

'Our berth on Staten Island is to be Pier 14,' announced the signalman.

'Thank you, Bunts,' said the captain. 'Did you get that, pilot?'

'Sure thing,' said the pilot. 'Our guys will be there to meet you. Things ain't been so good lately.'

He was right. Secured alongside it seemed that every member of American staff on the Island called on us, doing their best to make us welcome. That first afternoon found the entire crew sitting in the sun eating American ice cream. Of course, there was some latent competition between us and the Americans – above all we wanted to win the war and it would be splendid if we could show the Yanks how to do it. Despite the friendly welcome, many in the United States Navy had grave doubts that our squadron, a motley collection of fishing boats, trawlers, drifters and whalers, could be of real help in combating Hitler's U-boats. An attitude summed up by a US Coast Guard sailor who looked down on *Wastwater* from the quay and called out, 'Say, did you guys really cross the Atlantic in that thing?'

On the second day the captain and first lieutenant of both our ships were invited to visit US Navy headquarters in Church Street. They were greeted with great friendliness and Commander Pierce, who was to be our operational chief, gave a business-like outline of the situation and the tasks he had planned for us. Before any of that, though, with typical American thoroughness, our ships were to be checked for defects in Brooklyn Dockyard. The speed at which the dockyard men worked was extraordinary.

'They don't hang around like you bloody lot,' said the coxswain, addressing the crew at the 0800 divisions.

'Ah,' said our signalman, 'that's because they get paid.'

The dockyard supervisor was appalled by our antique four-pounder. 'I'll get you a new gun,' he said, 'and I'll change it right away.'

That afternoon his men began dismantling our old firing-piece. But the following morning orders came through that we were to keep the old gun. I never did find out who had put a stop to the work, some wretched clerk in the Admiralty probably. Still, the junior member of our gun crew was delighted. 'I'll look after her properly,' he told me, 'she's a nice old thing.'

During the short refit there was a bonus – four days' leave for everyone. Ship's company and officers were to be billeted ashore, the officers in the Barbers and Plaza Hotel, close to Central Park. Junior officers had to share a room, but lieutenants and above had one of their own.

'What's your name?' I was asked at reception.

'Lieutenant Holder-Jones,' I replied, keeping the solitary ring on my cuffs out of sight. Actually, it wasn't such a big lie – my promotion was due. But perhaps by the grand age of 27 I had finally acquired a bit of 'savvy' as the American called it.

Staying at the Barbers and Plaza in the centre of Manhattan gave us a marvellous opportunity to explore New York. America is an extraordinarily vibrant, powerful and generous nation. I had wondered about the substantial German and Italian communities living in the city. We were fighting their countries, and yet in New York we were friends.

One well-dressed man approached me and said, in a loud voice, 'Damn your king.'

'And damn your president,' I replied, whereupon he laughed and invited me to join him in a drink.

Some asked why we were allowing General Rommel to push us around in North Africa. But everywhere there was admiration for the way the British people were standing up to the blitz and the German bombs. Some of us, visiting the seaman's mission, were astonished to see there a number of the cruelly frostbitten

American sailors *Wastwater* had rescued off Greenland.

It was at the Barbers and Plaza that I began to appreciate the kindness and friendship that our hosts were extending to all British seamen. An evening out at the theatre, a restaurant, 'come home and meet my folks', sightseeing, a day in the country – it was all there for enlisted men and officers alike.

Within a week our ships were released from the dockyard and returned to Pier 14. Our short holiday was over. The yard had done a marvellous job, they had even given us a water-cooler, a real bonus. Back on Staten Island we found great changes in Pier 14 too. It had a new workshop, well-equipped stores, a diner, a drink dispenser, and best of all, bathrooms and showers with unlimited hot water.

Commander Pierce wasted no time in putting us to work. There were two days of general drills when we were inspected by a group of American officers. We fired our guns, dropped our depth charges, exercised fire and emergency stations, 'Three men overboard,' and so it went on. I think the American officers were impressed, certainly with our Asdic ratings – 'much better than ours,' one of them whispered to me.

After some preliminary patrols we started a regular duty, escorting convoys between New York and Delaware. On the first morning we slipped from Staten Island at 0400 in company with *Buttermere* and steamed down the long channel to the sea, passing a multitude of buoys. At the entrance to the harbour we found our convoy forming up and we were hailed by a group of small US boats and launches asking us for instructions. It was extraordinary – after being the tail-end Charlies of convoys for so many months, we were in charge. For the first time I used some of the signalling procedures I had learnt on the battleship *Nelson*. We stationed our group of small boats according to their equipment and their number. Nervous at first, it was a job we came to enjoy.

On that first morning we had clear sunny weather, but there was a reminder of a previous Atlantic convoy when for the better part of three days we had struggled to keep a Greek ship in order. Mid-morning, *Wastwater* had to go alongside a tramp which despite orders had steamed on ahead.

'Slow down, slow down,' we shouted.

Then came a cheerful voice from the bridge, 'Sorry old boy, I don't understand your lingo, I'm a Greek.'

'It's always them Greeks that cause trouble,' said one of our lookouts. 'My sister married one and he's a fucking nightmare.'

To onlookers it might have seemed that we were enjoying a leisurely cruise down to the south, but we were conscious of the risks and disturbed by the number of wrecks we had to navigate, tankers and merchantmen that had been sunk in the previous months. I thought of the poor seamen caught below decks who would still be there – food for the crabs.

On our third convoy we had unexpected company. Almost without our noticing, an American coastguard blimp came alongside, flying just a little higher than our bridge.

'Say fellas, I've come to help you!' the blimp's captain called out through his loudhailer.

Our captain was aghast.

'Get rid of him, Jones! Any U-boat could spot us from miles away.'

Picking up the loudhailer, I replied, 'Thank you so much, captain. We think a U-boat may be following us. Could you please take station twenty miles astern.'

'Sure thing!' – and with that the blimp disappeared.

Just two hours later he was back.

'Say guys, it's rather lonely out there. But I've got to go now. I'm running out of fuel.'

Most days we could measure our progress from the various landmarks on the flat sandy shore – the water towers, groups of houses, and the tall buildings of Atlantic City. As a rule we delivered our convoys from New York to Delaware at around dusk. Sometimes we would anchor for the night but more usually we would go on patrol. Then we would wait for the next northbound ships. We would spend some four to five days at sea shepherding our different charges before returning to Staten Island to take on new stores, deal with defects and attend to a multitude of paperwork while waiting for our next set of sailing instructions.

Although we were worked hard, we were fortunate in having

time between our duties to catch the Staten Island Ferry to the Big Apple. The ferry was remarkable, and for just five cents it took us to another world. Tough, old-fashioned, punctual – I grew to love it and the people I met on board.

'Say, you boys sound different. Are you from the old country?' As often as not such a greeting would be followed by an invitation.

At the Barbers and Plaza Hotel I had been given an introduction to an unlikely friend – F E Johnson, an American oil millionaire. I spent several weekends with him. He was an extraordinary man, very rich but generous with no side. I used to join him on his train from Grand Central Station to New Jersey on Friday evenings –

'Geoffrey, you make yourself comfortable. Order anything you like. Me, I'm going to play cards with some friends – it's become a habit – but you stay put, the stakes are high. You don't find that rude, do you?'

'Of course not.'

He had a grand house, and on our arrival his wife would meet me on the front steps. Each time she would introduce me to Barbara, a friendly maid, who insisted on carrying my case as she took me to my room.

'Fancy a swim?' said F E, 'water's only 80, but I guess that's good for you guys.'

On the bed there would be a pair of bathing trunks and a thick white towel. And he was a thoughtful man in other ways. He had a workshop – 'It's yours to come and go as you wish, Geoffrey. I find that some of you lot really enjoy it. They can switch off and do something different – one of your guys made a chair. He said at the end of the war he would come and collect it. I hope he does.' Johnson was an Anglophile who loved London.

The family enjoyed entertaining, and there were always interesting visitors at the weekends – government officials, newspapermen, oilmen, sportsmen, diplomats, and politicians. As guests the after-dinner entertainment fell to us, though the Johnson family itself was a star turn. Four of F E's sons could sing and they joined together in a barbershop quartet. Still, It wasn't too difficult for me as I'd acquired some talent for writing poems in the manner of Stanley Holloway. But that first evening, taken by surprise, I forgot a couple of lines. Despite the generous applause I knew I could have done better. Next time I would be prepared.

In the spring of 1942 the war had hardly touched New York. Shop windows were full of goods, chocolates and fruit, restaurants displayed menus as long as your arm, and US sailors thought nothing of throwing away their half-smoked 'seegars'. From the start of our stay in New York we had been victualled by the US Navy. Suddenly, we were enjoying an extraordinary range of delicacies: chicken cooked in a hundred different ways, ice cream, fruit juices, Kellogg's cornflakes, pancakes and maple syrup, cold cuts, and liberal supplies of eggs, ham, lettuce and other vegetables. Mind you, many of the ship's company, with English stubbornness, preferred a roast, two veg, gravy and a liberal lump of duff.

But there was one problem in this near-paradise: our pay was but a fraction of that earned by American servicemen, and within a week most of us were very short of money. American officers were always taking us out to dinner. Early each month, while we were in funds, we would return the compliment. 'That's it for this month, folks,' we'd say, 'it's our treat next, first week of June.'

In July our two ships were ordered to proceed to the naval dockyard in Norfolk, Virginia, for a refit. Once again we followed *Buttermere*. Two miles outside the harbour entrance we had a signal: 'Man overboard, astern.' Although we were only a cable away we could see no sign of him. What could have happened? Had the poor devil gone straight to the bottom? Fouled a propeller? Another signal arrived, 'Man recovered!' The seaman had caught hold of the line towing the ship's log, a small contraption with an impeller which measured the ship's speed and distance run. He was hauled back on board, none the worse for wear.

In Norfolk the ship was in the care of the dockyard for two weeks, which meant each watch had a week's leave which we were to spend at a holiday camp. We were taken on tours of the magnificent Virginia countryside, its forests, places of interest and the university. One afternoon out we met two old ladies who served tea, sandwiches and scones in the English fashion. 'We like to make you English visitors feel at home.' The size of the Norfolk docks was extraordinary, and true to form the Americans worked at a rapid pace. Before long we were back in Staten Island and 'home'.

One day I had a marvellous reunion with Roland, my older brother. He was navigating officer of the *Aquitania*, a famous Atlantic liner which spent the war as a trooper carrying the better part of two thousand men, taking American troops to England and North Africa, Australian troops to Europe, English troops to the Far East and so on. New York was a regular stop for the *Aquitania* and Roland knew his way around.

I had wanted to go to Harlem but found difficulty in getting anybody who would join me. 'Will you take me?' I asked Roland.

He was doubtful. 'It'll be not what you think,' he said, 'but we'll go.'

We took the subway to Harlem. It was about 1900 in the evening and the whole place was as dead as a dodo with hardly anyone on the streets. We found a nightclub with just three girls, a barman and a band. We had a couple of dances with two of the black girls. Nice enough but it wasn't up to much, and feeling vaguely ridiculous we took the subway back into town and had dinner in Greenwich Village.

Our two days together were soon over. That last evening he asked what I would be doing when he sailed on the early morning tide.

'Oh, we'll be up before you,' I told him airily, 'and we'll clear the U-boats out of your way.'

And that's just what we did. On leaving the entrance of the harbour, *Aquitania* sped away from us like a greyhound, at a speed of some thirty knots. She was the most beautiful sight, her clean lines unimpaired despite her peeling paintwork. Ships like the *Aquitania* sailed without a convoy. Their very speed was their protection.

As well as escorting Allied convoys, we adopted an aggressive approach to our unseen foes. At the hint of a suspicious echo we would drop patterns of depth charges, and despite the initial fears of our hosts the number of sinkings was much reduced. Indeed, not that we boasted – well, perhaps just a little – neither *Buttermere* nor *Wastwater* lost a ship. Of course it was a great help when the American navy at last accepted that the British convoy system was the best way of protecting their ships. Their initial resistance had to some extent been a matter of national pride, as had the delay in introducing a blackout along the coast.

Now of course America with all its might would have survived the onslaught of the U-boats, but I and many others believe our squadron of twenty-four small ships won the battle for the USA in the spring and summer of 1942.

Later there was another crucial factor which acted for the Allied forces against the U-boat menace: the work of the British code breakers at Bletchley Park. Though we were not aware of their activity until after the war, the code breakers were an extraordinary collection of clever and committed people who, throughout the war, worked long hours in difficult conditions trying to break the German Enigma system. The breakthrough came on 30 October 1942. A British Ship, HMS *Petard*, attacked a German submarine, U559, in the eastern Mediterranean. The submarine, with its pressure hull cracked, surfaced. Neglecting to destroy their code books and their Enigma machine, the German crew scrambled overboard and took their chance in the water. Three British sailors, Able Seaman Colin Grazier, Lieutenant Francis Fasson and Canteen Assistant Tommy Brown, swam naked to the slowly sinking submarine and retrieved the Enigma machine and the code book which contained all the current settings for the U-boat Enigma key. Grazier and Fasson were inside the boat searching for more intelligence material when it finally sank. Both were drowned. Grazier and Fasson were awarded the George Cross and Brown, who had lied about his age on signing up, was the youngest ever recipient of the George Medal. The material rescued from the sinking U-boat was of immense value to the code breakers, who had been unable to read the U-boat Enigma for some nine months. It was the missing key that helped them crack the code. It has been calculated that the code breakers saved hundreds of ships and thousands of men in the latter stages of the war.

The next time I visited my friend F E Johnson, encouraged by Michael Thwaites I took a poem I had written about the Staten Island Ferry. I had a few drinks so I wasn't too nervous when my turn came to provide the entertainment. This time I didn't miss a line. It went down well. I got a round of applause.

Tale of the ferryboat that met a U-boat

I'll tell you a tale of a Ferryboat Captain,
Whose longest trip was Manhattan to Staten.

And this occupation I think you'll agree,
Ain't exciting enough if you're born to the sea.

Now he craved for adventure 'cause his life was so dull,
And he worried so much he was losing his wool.

So one starlit night 'e could stand it no longer;
He cried – " 'ard-a-port, George, let's see what's out yonder."

Now George 'e were 'elmsman, and held a clean ticket,
And breaking firm's rules; well it weren't playing cricket.

But he stood to his post; like Centurion of old,
Till his rose-budding nose, turned blue with the cold.

And Captain he smiled as he paced on the bridge,
Though the wind, through the swing doors made saloon like a fridge.

Now most of the passengers were beginning to worry;
They wanted to go home and were in rather a hurry.

But Captain was deaf, to their pleas and their cries;
And quoted some poetry, about seas and the skies.

And not to be outdone friend George beat the band,
With one about Nelson and old Pen-in-t'hand.

So the passengers soon settled down to their plight,
And made preparations for stopping the night.

They moved all drunks and rolled them on floor,
To help stop the wind blowing in under door.

Next morning, the sea had got a bit high,
And a nasty big cloud covered half of the sky.

But Captain stood there like a man in a dream,
Till George gave him a shove saying, "What's that on the beam?"

It were dirty big U-boat out on the prowl,
Complete with Commander, eyeglass and scowl.

But Captain kept cool; he'd been in worse spots,
And he bawled down the voice pipe for a dozen more knots.

Now the Chiefie he swore, 'cause his engines were knocking
And the language he used – was really quite shocking.

He was having some trouble with Big End and Straps,
And one of his stop valves was whistling Taps.

In meantime U-boat had been proper busy,
Firing torpedoes until he was dizzy.

But George he excelled in the art of his calling,
And evaded tin fish in a manner appalling.

So U-boat submerged to escape a collision.
It were, you'll agree, a wise sort of decision.

But Captain continued; he'd got an idea,
And swore if successful, he'd buy George a beer.

He hadn't no depth bombs, but he'd plenty of pluck;
So he opened the gates and dropped a 20-ton truck.

'Twas a good way of dealing with old Mr. Hun,
And provide all hands with plenty of fun.

So they forgot all their troubles, and raised a wild cheer.
And they all started talking of prize money and beer.

The Nazis were captured and taken on board.
And Commander gave Captain his gilt-hilted sword.

It were all very fancy, but really no use,
The blade were all chipped, and the handle was loose.

The Captain was pleased, and said – "Thanks very much sir,
If you're sure you don't mind I'll give it our butcher.

Happen he'll mend it, and sharpen the blade,
Then wave it at folks when their bills are unpaid."

Then the Captain decided the best thing to do,
Was to set sail for home and George thought so too.

But when ship was turned round, the Captain said – "Hey!
Believe me or not, George, I've forgotten the way."

But as fate would have it, their good luck held out;
One of the Bootblacks had been a Boy Scout.

He learned knots and splices, and plenty of tricks;
Such as lighting a fire by rubbing two sticks.

But 'twas in navigation he'd come out best,
By remembering Sun always set in West.

So they followed the Sun, for more than an hour –
Till someone on top sighted Parachute Tower.

And all the passengers ran to the side,
They all felt so happy that some of them cried.

An hour or so later they were safely on land,
A bit disappointed cause there wasn't a band.

But Ferry Inspector was waiting on stage.
He was looking for Captain and weren't half in a rage.

Crying – "Where have you been for the last day or so?"
And Captain, being truthful, said, "I really don't know.

But we've sunk old U-boat, and captured some Huns;
And invented a depth charge, that weighs 20 tons."

So a policeman was sent for, and they told him their tale,
The Huns were arrested and locked up in jail.

At last news of the exploit reached the ears of the Mayor,
Who arranged a reception to be held in Times Square.

And Captain was granted a lifelong desire.
To ride with the Mayor to the next City Fire.

The Bootblack got Boy Scout's Wayfarer's Star,
And George a half share in Jack Dempsey's Bar.

Then the Chiefie got medal for his daring and pluck,
And U-boat Commander – got the bill for the truck.

One of the guests, a newspaperman called Mackenzie, asked if he could have a copy. Mackenzie was a friend of Gracie Fields, and he suggested that Gracie might like to use my poem as part of her hugely successful concert tour. Sadly, it never came to pass – she thought the humour too British for an American audience – but I still have the very kind letter she sent Mackenzie.

CABLE ADDRESS: "WALDORF, NEW YORK" / ELDORADO 5-3000

The WALDORF-ASTORIA

PARK AND LEXINGTON AVENUES / 49TH AND 50TH STREETS / NEW YORK

October 13, 1942

Dear Mackenzie,

Thank you very much for giving me the poem written by your friend, Lieut. Geoffrey Holden Jones. It is very amusing but I am terribly sorry to have to disappoint you and say I'm afraid I won't be able to use it. You see, we understand dialect but the American public doesn't catch on to it quickly enough, and it's too long for me to use. Naturally, I don't want to tell you I will use it if I can't. I like to tell people straight if I can do a thing or not.

Back home, yes, it would be very handy, but please try and forgive me for having to disappoint you and your friend. If there is an opportunity for me to use it when I come across a more English audience than the Americans you can bet your life I will use it.

Best wishes.

Your sincere,

Gracie Fields

I thought no more about it until I received a call from the American magazine *Newsweek*.

'Hey, we'd like to print your poem. We'll pay you.' And they did! It appeared in the issue for 26 October 1942.

12

The Caribbean

After five months of escort duty, by which time I could name every wreck and buoy from New York to the Delaware, there was a sudden and extraordinary change to our duties. Our captain and the captain of the *Buttermere* were summoned to Church Street where they were given new orders by Commander Pierce to escort a floating dock from Boston to St Thomas in the Caribbean. It sounded like fun until we began to consider the logistics. The dock was an enormous piece of kit, the size of an ocean liner, but squat, clumsy and with a maximum towing speed of three and a half knots, a sitting duck for any submarine. And Boston to St Thomas was a very long way. It would take weeks to get her there. Would we and the dock last that long?

A few days later, on a hot summer's afternoon, we followed *Buttermere* out of the East River to sea, the Manhattan skyline to our port and Brooklyn to our starboard. I ducked as we went underneath the bridges. It's strange but going under a bridge has always given me a moment of apprehension. Of course I knew there was enough room – it was my job to check – but approaching a bridge, instinctively my head went down. The captain was amused but too polite to say anything. We passed the streets of Manhattan, only a hundred yards away, and stared at the New Yorkers while they stared at us. What did they make of two tiny British warships flying the white ensign? Our signalman caught sight of the commander of engineering, the senior British officer in charge of our squadron. He'd come to see us off, and by semaphore he wished us luck.

We came across the dock at dusk. She had two tugs, one British and one American, and we took station on either beam, steering an irregular zigzag. Oddly I soon began to think of the dock, clumsy, ungainly creature that she was, with some affection. At dawn, or coming on watch, the first thing I would do was look and make sure she was still with us. Would her luck and ours hold? There were still enemy submarines about. Just one submarine could be our undoing. On the other hand, below the waves, enemy U-boats could hear the sound of our Asdics. The ping and echo of an approaching escort would stretch the nerves of the enemy submariners. They knew that our depth charges were every bit as effective as a destroyer's.

The dock was manned by a British chief petty officer with a small crew whose main job was to operate the pumps and to watch the towing hawsers. The pumps were important because while the dry dock was in tow it would ship copious amounts of water. Through our binoculars we could see the dock's crew sunbathing on the superstructure. An easy life? Hardly. We did not envy them, not one bit. In the event of an attack they would be lucky to survive.

As we edged south the weather became warm and ever more humid. But there were compensations – flying fish, and porpoises swimming in perfect formation just ahead of our bow wave. It was almost as if there was a friendship between the ship, the porpoises and our crew. As the porpoises weaved patterns and surfed alongside I heard two of our stokers talking about them –

'They're bloody great, they are,' declared one.

'They're fucking marvellous,' agreed the other.

And so they were. We also now had a shower – luxury! The crew had rigged a saltwater shower on deck and a night watch was a pleasure, clean and dressed in a pair of shorts and a shirt with the stars for company. Michael, our first lieutenant, was meticulous in insisting that we kept a good watch and blacked out our lights.

Seven days out and we had developed a love/hate relationship for 'our dock'. It still wallowed behind the tugs and it was so very, very slow. Periodically the Asdic would make a contact – 'Action stations!' I would rush to the four-inch. A submarine would be easier to hit than an aircraft and a hit would make us heroes. But always it was another false alarm, yet another whale!

As we edged towards St Thomas there were more and more thunderstorms. In an instant a blue sky would change to black, then lightning, the crash of thunder and then rain, or 'more stair rods' as the signalman so aptly put it. I preferred the tropics to the North Atlantic, but the *Wastwater* had been built for colder seas and in the heat and humidity our mess decks became unbearable. To think that we had once plugged the ventilators with sacking to keep warm! Still we began to learn a new way of life. We stopped the mess decks being flooded by torrential rain by hoisting a sail to divert water over the side. There was an added bonus to that, as the sail provided some shade when the sun was out. Of course we had our two refrigerators, which at least stopped our butter from melting, but *Wastwater* remained an exceedingly hot steel box by day and by night.

The tugs were responsible for navigation, so we would take our noon position with our sextants and compare our position with theirs. Slowly the crosses on the chart edged southwards towards a dot marked St Thomas. To make a landfall is always an exciting moment, and for most of us this would be our first sight of the West Indies.

The captain had promised a tot of rum to the first man to see the island's lighthouse.

'There's a light, sir, just off the starboard bow.'

'Light flashing off the port bow, sir.'

'That's a star.'

And so we steamed on and still there was no light. Was our noon position wrong? There was an air of gloom about the ship. It seemed that we were to have another day at sea. Later the answer became clear – as a wartime precaution the strength of St Thomas's light had been reduced from twenty miles to six.

Our arrival was a great moment. We slowly steamed through the strait between St Thomas and Sail Rock. It was a warm, peaceful night with the gentlest of breezes. The whole scene was drenched in moonlight and in front of us loomed the dark outlines of the St Thomas mountains while the light we had all been looking for flashed on our beam. It was a night to remember. As dawn came we rounded Sail Rock and we saw the island of St Thomas from the south. The signal station onshore began to talk to us, and our Aldis replied. We were instructed to remain on patrol until the dock was safely anchored, after which were to proceed into harbour. We had an extraordinary sense of relief. The job was done and our dock was now someone else's responsibility. Later we learnt about her end. Escorted by an armed merchant cruiser bound for South Africa, she had run into heavy weather in the South Atlantic. The seas broke her up and she had to be abandoned – the end of a very expensive voyage. Later still I was told that we been 'protected' by the Germans. Naval intelligence had learnt that the German Admiral Dönitz had instructed U-boat commanders to keep their torpedoes for use against larger merchant ships, and in particular tankers.

We didn't stay long in St Thomas. Our next job was to escort a convoy of six ships to Key West, the American naval base at the tip of Florida. But before the convoy arrived *Wastwater* was detached to escort a small tanker loaded with diesel fuel to Santo Domingo. President Rafael Trujillo had renamed the capital city after himself, and why not? He was both President and Generalissimo, an old-fashioned Latin American despot. To his credit, though, the dictator had sided with the Allies in the war. By way of revenge German submarines immediately sank his entire fleet of two ships. Consequently, Ciudad Trujillo, without its normal supply of diesel, faced a total blackout. We delivered our charge without mishap and proceeded slowly up the river to the capital. There were some imposing buildings and a huge national flag floated over a high turreted building. It took us a moment before we realised it was a prison. We could see cells with vertical iron bars. Behind them, watching us, were hundreds of prisoners wearing shirts with horizontal stripes. 'No doubt liberty men who outstayed their leave,' joked the first lieutenant. Our sailors grinned, but a little uneasily.

An enormous crowd, who appeared to be waiting to greet us, were gathered on a modern quay in the centre of the city.

'The last British navy ship here, in 1938, was the cruiser *Cumberland*,' the pilot explained. I remembered the cinema and the impressive wardroom. Whatever will they make of us, I wondered.

Well, we still had our Victorian gun, and I resolved to ask one of our gun crew to give it an extra polish. We came alongside in an area where the police had cleared the crowds and were hardly secured before officials crossed a swaying gangway and jumped on board. Within minutes the whole of the foredeck was swarming with visitors, saluting, shaking hands and wishing us well.

If the locals were disappointed with the size of our ship they were too polite to mention it, and for the whole of our stay we were treated as heroes. Our captain, as the guest of the British minister, was taken on several official visits including an impressive reception hosted by the Generalissimo's brother, who greeted him with a guard of honour while a band played martial music. In his turn the British minister hosted a banquet which according to the captain was notable for its excellent wine and a great deal of ceremonial hand-kissing. While the captain was enjoying the high life the first lieutenant and I were entertained by our legations secretary, Mr Smithy, and his American wife. Despite an acute shortage of petrol, they, together with their two small boys, took us on a splendid tour of the island and we whiled away a marvellous evening sipping rum and coke and shooting tins. A little drunk, I spent rather too much of the evening quoting my Lancashire recitations, but they didn't seem to mind. As for the crew, the Smithys organised cinema outings and swimming parties. The Dictator Trujillo had staged a right royal reception for us.

Santo Domingo – now the Dominican Republic – comprises two-thirds of the large oblong West Indies island of Hispaniola, the other third being Haiti. It was this island that Christopher Columbus made famous, and where he lies buried in the cathedral. And, it was from San Domingo that both Cortés and Pizarro launched their expeditions and discovered the New World.

It was a strange but enjoyable time for us. There we were flying the flag of democracy in a foreign country, honoured guests of a Latin American dictator. Not, perhaps, the tour of duty that Winston Churchill had envisaged when he lent our squadron of assorted fishing boats to President Roosevelt. But it was a welcome break from our regular routine, and *Wastwater* and her crew surely deserved it. While the Generalissimo was a dictator it has to be said that on the surface at least his people seemed content, even happy. Another remarkable fact which we all noticed was the cleanliness of the public buildings, the monuments and the streets. This cleanliness and order was unusual in the West Indies and was entirely down to the Generalissimo of the Armed Services, Benefactor of the Fatherland and Restorer of Independence, who didn't like litter. Indeed, litter bugs were sometimes shot, or at the very least sent to prison. The Generalissimo lived in great personal luxury and ruled the republic with ruthlessness and efficiency. On the other hand, the country's products of sugar, salt and matches were exported to the USA and Britain. More than that, the Generalissimo had declared war against Germany and, to his great credit, Santo Domingo was one the few countries in the world that welcomed Jews who had fled the Nazi tyranny.

Leaving Trujillo, we rejoined *Buttermere* and together escorted six merchant ships to Key West. The weather was fine, and steering along the north coast of Cuba we had a comfortable passage. On the final morning we caught sight of another convoy far away on the northern horizon, the merchant ships and their escorts clearly visible. As we watched, a column of water shot into the air close to one of the merchant ships and then subsided. A moment later the same thing happened to another ship, followed by two audible thuds. The ships in the convoy plodded on as the escorts moved hither and thither searching for their underwater foe. That evening we berthed in Key West and were given the details. Both ships had sunk in a few minutes, together with their cargoes and a heavy loss of life.

But it wasn't all bad, for there was good news for our first lieutenant. He had a cable from Honor, his wife, telling him of the safe arrival of his new son Peter. We had a congratulatory dinner and drank rather too much. I went to sleep that night thinking of Gladys.

The following day I was miserable and upset. It wasn't a hangover. The sinking of the two American ships had brought back memories I had hidden away, and I told my colleagues for the first time what had really happened when my ship, *Adventure*, had been torpedoed. It all came flooding out, the terror and the bloodstained corpses, the inky blackness below decks and the ship listing to one side.

From Key West it was back to New York. It should have been an easy voyage, but the weather turned and the wind blew in from the north. For three days we sailed in bitter cold across heaving seas. 'I wanted to die,' said one of our new officers who had suffered from severe seasickness. South of Delaware, we gave a tow to a small yacht – God alone knows how she survived the storm. On the fifth day, battered and bruised, we made it back to Pier 14, Staten Island. It was like arriving home, but it wouldn't be for long. After a few short escort duties, *Wastwater* was given sailing instructions to escort a six-ship convoy to Bermuda. As for me, I received orders to join HMS *Baffin* as first lieutenant. *Baffin* was a new ship berthed in Montreal. Back to the snow and ice, I grumbled. Still, a promotion was a promotion, and it was time to move on. I was given a marvellous farewell party and the crew even bought me a clock. It was with tears in my eyes that I bade them farewell.

13

Canada

Winter came early to New York in 1942. A little sad after saying goodbye to my shipmates on *Wastwater*, I headed for Grand Central Station. It was snowing and unseasonably cold. In one hand I had a first-class railway warrant to Montreal, in the other a battered cardboard suitcase and a tennis bag. I was tired, feeling ill and apprehensive. I had spent the better part of two years on *Wastwater* without any real break. Being third officer can be more onerous than being captain or first lieutenant. I kept thinking about Gladys. The last thing I really wanted was to go to Montreal and join another trawler. But help was at hand.

Finally, I clambered onto the train after checking a couple of times to make sure I was on the right one and sat down in a deserted first-class compartment. But before the train left I was joined by a Canadian lumberjack, six feet tall – well, nearer seven – and big to go with it. He told me a bit about himself and, saying he had something to share with me, produced a bottle of vodka from his coat pocket.

'I've got some more tucked away,' he assured me.

Well, I have never been adverse to a drink. So while the snow grew deeper each stop, in a haze of alcohol, reasonable seats and a comfortable bunk at night, our two-day train ride was soon over. The lumberjack's stories of taking timber down great rivers were fascinating, but he was a lonely man desperate for company and love. I realised how lucky I was that I had Gladys, however far away she was.

On arrival at Montreal I said goodbye to my lumberjack and

began to search for HMS *Baffin*. Remembering my struggles to find *Wastwater*, it came as no surprise when I was told my ship was now in Quebec. The naval staff at Montreal were kind, helpful and determined to ensure that I had the necessary clothing to combat the arctic winter.

'Oh I'll be alright, I survived Iceland and the North Atlantic.'

'It's a damn sight colder this side,' said one of the senior pursers – and he was right. I was given a fur hat and some overshoes, which proved invaluable.

I was put up in Montreal for a couple of days while being briefed. I then took a train to Quebec. The journey passed without incident, and on arrival I reported to the Navy Office where I was interviewed by the senior officer.

'Your captain has been taken ashore. I'm sorry to say he's seriously ill and he won't be back.' Looking me in the eye, he asked me if I'd be happy to sail the *Baffin* to Halifax.

'Of course sir, that'll be no problem.'

I realised that I was eager to see my new ship. Clearly the train journey had restored both my health and my spirits. It was cold, very cold, and I wondered about my lumberjack – there would be no work for him in such weather.

I caught a taxi to where *Baffin* was moored. She looked in good order – a brand new Admiralty class anti-submarine minesweeping trawler. On deck, Archie Hodge, an RNVR lieutenant who was to be my first lieutenant, was waiting to greet me. Immediately we met I knew we would get on, and my new ship had a good feel to it, with a friendly and experienced crew. Three days later I received sailing instructions for Halifax, Nova Scotia. There were already ice floes on the Saint Lawrence and ice round the ship. I was nervous and couldn't rid myself of the ridiculous notion that the ice might hold the *Baffin* to the side of the jetty.

In the event all went well, and on clearing the harbour and reaching open water my first lieutenant spoke: 'Well done captain!'

Captain – that sounded good. I determined to make the best of my time in command. *Baffin* handled well but was nothing like as manoeuvrable as dear old *Wastwater*, which could turn on a sixpence.

After five hours steaming the chief engineer came to the bridge looking worried. 'Trouble sir, I'm afraid. Our main shaft is out of alignment.'

'Can you fix it ?' I asked.

He shook his head. 'I'm afraid not, sir. It's a dockyard job.'

'How long?'

'Two, three weeks, maybe a month.'

I was horrified. Was my time in command to be spent with dockyard engineers crawling all over the ship? The chief led me below to the engine room. When revolutions increased I could hear the unwelcome sound of a knock.

'Can you get us to Halifax, chief?' I couldn't bear the thought of returning to Quebec the moment after taking command.

'Aye, if you take things easy,' he replied.

Back on the bridge, I looked at the charts and once more was amazed at the length and size of the St Lawrence River with its rocks and sandbanks. What seamanship and navigation skills our sailors had shown nearly two hundred years previously when they had taken General Wolfe's army from Louisburg to Quebec. Some two hundred sailing ships had transported the army over eight hundred miles. Later, in the dead of night, these seamen had taken their ships through the Quebec narrows to anchor beneath the Heights of Abraham where Wolfe landed his troops and led them up the cliffs. There was a short but decisive battle and the city was captured. Wolfe lost his life but became a national hero. During my short stay in Quebec I had visited the battleground and wondered again at Wolfe's remarkable and unlikely victory.

I too had my own small victory. Five days after leaving Quebec we limped into Halifax with our shaft knocking ever louder. I am not sure that ships can limp but that's how it felt. *Baffin* was sent straight to the dockyard for repair and there we were to remain for the better part of a month. The dockyard mateys seemed less than interested.

'We'd have been better off in Glasgow,' grumbled the chief engineer, 'they just sit in the warm and do sweet fuck all.'

He was right. I was furious and remonstrated in no uncertain terms. But nothing happened, there was no sense of urgency.

Well, something did happen – the following morning the dockyard supervisor arrived on board agitated and angry. 'For God's sake, Jones, watch your language or there will be a strike.'

There was nothing for it. I swallowed my pride and apologised. Then another indignity. I received a top secret message in a brown paper envelope. In naval fashion the first envelope contained a second brown envelope stamped TOP SECRET. The contents of the second envelope informed us that four Russian submarines under the command of a Russian admiral were to berth alongside. The *Baffin* was instructed to provide steam for the submarines. Usual courtesies were to be observed but on no account were any of the Russians to be shown round our ship.

Two days later the submarines arrived. I went to greet them and asked the admiral politely if I might entertain him.

'Niet.'

Was there perhaps any other way I could assist?

'Niet.'

The *Baffin* and the submarines both posted sentries, but even our sailors, garrulous and curious as they were, could not get a word from the Russian sailors. It was rather sinister. Five days later, when (or so we assumed) the submarines had been provisioned, re-armed and defects repaired, the small fleet of Russian submarines left us.

'I am glad the Niets have gone,' said Archie. We never did find out anything about our silent guests.

Still, our enforced stay in Halifax had its compensations. It gave us time to explore the city. The captain of destroyers, Captain D as he was known, ran a well-attended dance every Saturday, and dinner at the Nelson Hotel was good fun. Alcohol was prohibited but nevertheless readily available. The hotel had a working arrangement with the local police – at 10.00 pm precisely the police would arrive, check there was no alcohol on the table, which of course there wouldn't be, and then leave until the next evening. Home-made hooch was everywhere too and could be lethal. Our first lieutenant, who ashore led a complicated love life, would warn the crew on a regular basis about the dangers of illegal alcohol, but we never had any trouble on that score.

Halifax was a very different place from New York, but its people were just as friendly and many of our crew became regular guests at local family dinner tables. And I, too, was fortunate in meeting Ellen and her family who had moved to Halifax from Brazil. I spent several weekends as their guest. A night ashore in a home was a real treat – no generators, no need to shout above the noise of engines. Deep sleep, peace and a leisurely breakfast was something to cherish. Ellen and I kept in touch for many years, and once she came to London. Much later she returned to Brazil. 'I couldn't bear the cold in Nova Scotia,' she told me.

In Halifax the great explosion of 1917 was very much on people's minds. In the middle of another great war the fear was that history would repeat itself. In 1917 a French munitions ship had collided with a Norwegian freighter and caused the biggest man-made explosion the world had seen and would see before Hiroshima. Two thousand people had been killed, nine thousand injured and tens of thousands made homeless. We were shown the shadow of a man imprinted on a wall and part of an anchor blown two miles inland.

In some respects Halifax was like Iceland, but colder. A hard place to live, grim granite mountains and extremes of weather with icy gales that would blow for days. There were some advantages in the freezing conditions, though, with the inland lakes providing marvellous skating for young and old. Ice hockey, not football, was the game young men played.

One day, walking on Bedford Lake, I noticed four Christmas trees enclosing a small patch of open water. And there was an iceman – that's what they were called – carving foot-square blocks of ice. I was curious.

'I take the ice to my barn,' the man explained, 'where I cover it with a bit of straw. It'll last for the better part of a year, and in the summer I deliver it to my customers.'

Once it had been pointed out to me, I realised that almost every house in Halifax had an ice store, usually a small wooden structure adjoining the house.

'It's not a bad living, but it's hard work,' said the iceman.

'But the raw material comes free,' I remarked.

The iceman smiled.

One day I had a great surprise. *Wastwater* entered harbour and my friend Michael Thwaites came to see us. His book, *The Jervis Bay*, was doing well, and I was able to tell him that I had received one hundred and thirty dollars from *Newsweek*.

He chided me for jumping the queue in the promotion stakes: 'I'm senior to you and here you are captain of a new ship.'

'Oh, they'll find somebody to take over as soon as we are out of the bloody dockyard,' I told him.

We spent an evening together, and the following day *Wastwater* sailed off, escorting a small convoy of ships for Bermuda. We said goodbye, both wondering silently how the other would get on and hoping we would meet again.

By the time *Wastwater* arrived in Bermuda it was Christmas. *Baffin* was still stuck in Halifax. Nevertheless it was Christmas Eve, so I hung a stocking on the doorknob of my cabin. The following morning it was full to the brim, an apple, an orange, a card, odd bits of food and, delving to the bottom, the giblets of a turkey. Everybody had a good time. It was marvellous how our crew, a real mixed bunch, some Canadian, some Scottish, some English, and a few from Newfoundland, got on. Our officers too were excellent: Archie Hodge, our first lieutenant, had previously worked for Brylcreem, and Derek Hitchman, our navigator, was a schoolmaster and an excellent musician. When we went ashore he would seek out instruments to play, usually church organs. And then there was a young Canadian from Calgary who, despite having an air of perpetual astonishment, fitted in with our way of life. Mind you, he had to put up with some teasing when he told us that before joining our ship he had never seen the sea, but that didn't matter as there were plenty of lakes round Calgary. He had another difficulty – he never seemed to understand the difference between a penny and a cent. I am afraid some of our men took him for a ride. Still that Christmas was a great day which I will always remember. Perhaps the extreme cold and the shared danger had something to do with it, but there was a bond between us which I treasured and still do.

Finally out of dockyard hands, we went to the coaling jetty. We took on board 160 tons of coal. It was simply dumped on our deck and the dust spread everywhere, a film of the stuff that wouldn't go away. That day, the day of our coaling, there was a frost of minus twenty degrees Celsius. As a result, almost every pipe in our ship fractured. The mess was indescribable.

After coaling it was back to work, sea trials and working up to make sure the *Baffin* and her crew were ready for war. Then came the inevitable message – a new captain had been appointed to *Baffin* and would arrive that very evening.

Sure enough, late afternoon an RNR lieutenant arrived carrying a case.

'I have come to take command,' he told me.

'Shall I take your case to your cabin, sir?'

'No, leave it on deck for the moment. When do you sail for the UK?'

'Not in the foreseeable future, sir. We have orders that we are to escort the old St Lawrence ferry following the torpedoing of the *Caribou*.'

'So there are no plans to return to England?'

'None that I know of,' I replied.

'Well that's no good to me, I can't stand the cold.'

And with that he disappeared into the night. An extraordinary conversation. At base the following morning I was asked whether the new commanding officer had arrived.

'Yes,' I replied, 'but he didn't seem to like the look of us. He, well, he left.'

'Well then, you'd better take over.'

A few days later my appointment was confirmed. And that is how I became captain of one of His Majesty's ships.

Battleship Baffin
They called her
Pride of the Northern Seas
A smart little craft
Like a waterlogged raft
But she is all
The world to me

After helping assemble several convoys, *Baffin* was detached and we began escorting the SS *Snaefell*, an old St Lawrence ferry which had been brought out of retirement. By that time I had pinned a hat badge on the fur hat I had been given at Montreal. I remembered how cavalier I had been about the cold. I hadn't known what cold was. The Western side of the North Atlantic is indeed a damn site colder than the east, and on the open bridge my fur hat made an enormous difference. The old ferry did well enough, but wherever she went she made clouds of black smoke.

'A submarine could see us miles away,' Archie grumbled.

I'm pleased to report that, nevertheless, the *Snaefell* survived the war. The winter of 1942/3 was exceptionally cold, and navigating the stretch of water into Sydney and Port aux Basques was often hazardous. The ice, in particular round Port aux Basques, was thick and dangerous. We learnt to look for patches of open water, and of course we had the good sense to follow the ferry – she knew the way. In addition to our ferry escort duty, *Baffin*, together with three other ships, patrolled the Cabot Straits, the mouth of the St Lawrence River. We often stopped at Sydney, a very busy industrial town with coal mines and one of the largest steel works in the world. The mines and the steel works were in large part manned by a native tribe, the Anticosti, some of whom changed into full native dress at weekends. I have a picture of them – they were fine-looking men.

As winter began to ease its grip we were conscious that the theatre of war had moved into the mid Atlantic, where U-boat packs and our convoys continued their grim struggle. Occasionally we would be given other work, to escort ships to St John's or Bowaters at Corner Brook. There were different diversions too, anti-submarine exercises with an old K class submarine which was used as a target. But after some months with no action and no sight of the enemy I was conscious that boredom could become a problem. Too much waiting around is bad for morale. Archie, an excellent organiser, took the lead. The crew was kept busy – a fishing party, a visit to see the French fortifications in Louisburg, the largest in the New World, a day spent sealing with the Port aux Basques harbour master, a ride on Port aux Basques' remarkable train, the Newfoundland Flyer, an exercise involving a landing party with live ammunition on some desolate coast. We organised ship's dances when we were in Sydney, and all in all we had fun and some happy days. Still, by the autumn of 1943 I was thinking about leave. I had been away from the UK for nearly two years, and before that had spent the better part of a year in Iceland.

It was without much hope that I applied for leave to return to the UK. To my surprise my request was granted.

'Your first lieutenant, is he fit to take over command?' asked Naval Manning in Montreal.

I told them he would be excellent, and to my delight he was appointed. My ship would be in good hands and I could leave with a clear conscience. Perhaps even more surprisingly, my journey home was easy too. A sister ship, HMS *Cape Portland*, another trawler, was in Sydney when I got news of my leave. *Portland* was under orders to escort a convoy to Liverpool and the captain, a friendly man, offered me a berth. I volunteered to keep watch but the captain turned me down.

'Have a rest,' he told me kindly, 'and be our guest.'

Portland was part of the escort of a large well-organised convoy, but it took us an age – sixteen instead of eight days – to get home. The problem was that there were packs of U-boats reported in the mid Atlantic and the convoy was given continual alterations of course in order to avoid them. One night there was an attack. Convoy escorts fired hundreds of star shells into the air. The whole area was lit up with what seemed like millions of snow flakes, leaving the U-boats threading their way into our convoy with no place to hide. We were finally winning the war against our hidden foes.

It was the second week of January 1944 when at last we made fast in Wallasey. I jumped ship, caught the ferry across the Mersey, and got myself to Lime Street station in record time. There was a lot of bomb damage and the city was shabby, grey and down at heel. I rang Gladys. She wasn't there, she was on duty at the fire station, but I told her mother I was on the way. Needless to say my train was late. Twice it steamed in and out of Crewe station, and while trying to remember the rhyme about the junction I fell asleep. I woke up with that old song running around my head –

Oh Mr Porter, whatever shall I do?
I want to go to Birmingham but they've sent me on to Crewe.

But it wasn't Crewe, it was Euston. I was nearly home.

14

Blighty

It was strange, sitting in the train waiting for it to make its final move into Euston station. Canada and America seemed a million miles away. Had I really been away for two whole years? But now I was back in Blighty. The guard had hurried down the train telling everybody there would be a delay due to heavy traffic and a signal failure.

A well-dressed woman in the carriage, whom I judged to be well-off, commented, 'It's not the bloody Germans who are to blame, it's the signalmen.'

'Why the signalmen?' I asked.

'You heard the man. It wouldn't be the driver, they are far too sensible. My grandfather is a train driver.'

'Oh. Is he still driving?'

'Of course. He's far too old but he is doing his bit. Where have you come from?'

'Canada.'

'Lots of snow?'

The train lurched forward and that was the end of our conversation. I smiled, I was home.

Despite the late hour London was busy. Troops everywhere, American, Australian, Canadian and Indian adding to the mix. Bars, clubs and theatres were open, but despite the surface gaiety there was still a blackout and London was worn and tired, sandbags everywhere, empty buildings and then nothing at all save for a pile of bricks. I waited at a taxi rank.

'It's no good wasting your time waiting,' said an army captain.

'The Yanks have got the lot.'

It was not until ten o'clock the following morning that I finally got to Brighton and approached Gladys's parents' house in Moulsecoomb. Albert and Ethel were really nice people but it was over two years since we had last met and I was apprehensive. Gladys and I were to be married in three days' time, and apart from getting my brother Robert, who was on leave from his ship, to be my best man, I had done absolutely nothing. But I need not have worried. Ethel took charge.

'I'll give you some breakfast and then you can have a rest. Gladys's shift at the Preston fire station doesn't end till 1600 and Albert won't be back from the water board until later. We keep service time here you know, and Gladys is a leading fire officer,' she said proudly. 'We had begun to wonder whether you would arrive – we are so pleased to see you.' She could not have been kinder.

Gladys rushed into the house a little after 1600. All was well, and everything had been arranged. We were to be married in St Peter's Church on the Level, and afterwards there would be a reception at the Tatler in the Old Steine. Robert and I had booked into the Clarence Hotel in North Street for the three nights before the wedding, which happened to be on the day of Burns night – 25 January 1944. Gladys took me to St Peter's to meet the vicar, Geoffrey Ward, only to be met by the curate.

'Geoffrey is ill, I'm afraid, but I can play the organ and marry you at the same time.'

The day of our wedding dawned. Standing next to my brother Robert, I waited nervously for Gladys to arrive. She had been put back on night duty at the fire station and they had refused to give her even one night off. She wasn't due to finish her shift until 0800 on our wedding day. I couldn't help looking round, and I was surprised at the number of people who had come to the church to wish us well and pray for us. At last the triumphal music and Gladys. She looked marvellous, but underneath my best no. 1 jacket I was uncomfortable. For some reason I was suffering from dermatitis, and hard as I had tried I had been unable to get rid of the affliction.

The curate played his part to perfection. Periodically we were left at the altar while he played some of our favourite hymns, including 'Love divine, all love excelling,' before returning to the altar a little short of breath. His rushing from one post to the other made everyone smile and added to the occasion. Afterwards it was on to the Tatler, where the staff did us proud.

That evening we left for London. I remember overhearing one of our guests, 'That was a right good do.'

Better still, in London I had Gladys to myself. We were in love.

After our stay in London we spent the next ten days in the Blossoms Hotel in Chester. It was the wrong time of the year, wet and very windy, and I was thankful I was not at sea. But it was good to have the chance to introduce Gladys to my father, friends and relations, and she loved the views from the castle walls, which we walked whenever the gales relented. Sadly I was not as well as I should have been for my honeymoon and my dermatitis grew worse – so much so that I went to the military hospital in Eaton Hall. I was told to take two baths a day but that was no damn good so after our return to Brighton with Gladys back at her duties at the fire station I checked into the Saint Catherine's Lodge Hotel, which had become the sick bay for HMS *King Alfred*. I spent a week there being covered with some evil-smelling ointment, and when that didn't work, feeling really ill by now, I was transferred to the Royal Naval Hospital Hasler in Gosport.

'It's your diet,' a doctor told me. 'If you had been sailing with Captain Cook he would have recognised the problem immediately – you are suffering from a lack of vitamin C. It's scurvy. And what soap are you using?'

'Lux, the soap of the stars,' I told him.

'The worst possible choice,' he grunted.

So, a change of diet, vitamin C, lime juice, cabbage and the occasional orange and I was cured. Gladys was pleased. She was pretty fed up with me looking like a wreck and I couldn't blame her. I had not been a pretty sight and I knew it.

My leave over, I was appointed as an auxiliary naval pilot responsible to the King's Harbour Master at Portsmouth. I reported for duty.

'It's good to see you, Jones. We are very busy. You will work twenty-four hours on and twenty-four hours off. We will give you a cabin – here is a key. Go to the end of the corridor – it's the last door on the left. Come back in an hour and we will go over your duties.'

I walked down the corridor and opened the door. To my astonishment the room had no roof. I went back to the harbour master's office.

As soon as he saw my face he apologised. 'Sorry Jones, I had forgotten about the raid. But my assistant knows of some suitable digs in Southsea.'

The landlady, Mrs Everest, was a terrible old snob and only took me in when she was assured that as well as being a pilot I was also an officer.

The harbour master was right. All of us pilots were kept very busy. Portsmouth and all the waterways round the Isle of Wight, including Beaulieu River, were full of landing craft and small ships being made ready for the invasion of Normandy. In addition to those a large number of other ships had to enter Portsmouth for repair and provisioning. As an auxiliary pilot it was my responsibility to make sure that they reached the right berth at the right time and in safety. Easier said than done, as there were many commanding officers who for the first time were handling ships of some one hundred and fifty feet or more. Landing craft could be pigs to handle, shallow-drafted and slow to respond, and in any kind of a wind they would sheer all over the place. Pilots were not on board to take charge but to give advice – and even comfort when things got difficult.

I was surprised that there were few enemy air raids, but on one occasion a German sortie brought near-disaster. I was assisting a landing craft coming into Portsmouth, a large LCT, when there was an air raid warning. On an alert being sounded, every ship that could would make black smoke.

Despite the smoke we were on course and comfortable enough, when our bridge lookout shouted, 'Ship dead ahead, sir!'

The captain and I rushed to the voice pipe. 'Starboard ten.'

Right ahead was a large merchant ship. Somehow we managed to avoid the bows of the oncoming ship but scraped down its side.

There were sparks, great flashes from tearing metal, a smell of burning and a deafening noise. Just a few feet closer and we could have been turned over.

The merchantman sailed on to God knows where, but I had to complete the reams of paper work which the Admiralty demanded after a collision, however minor. Strangely enough I heard no more about the scrape – though thinking about it there would have been more crashes and bangs going on in the Solent than could be counted. I did make a recommendation. On landing craft the bridge, the wheelhouse and everything else was right aft, so I put in a report suggesting that it would be sensible if a lookout were stationed on the bow, particularly in poor visibility.

'A good idea,' said the harbour master – but I don't know that anybody took any notice.

As D-Day approached more and more landing craft arrived in Portsmouth and we had nowhere to put them, despite exploring Hasler Creek, the water round HMS *Excellent* and anywhere else we could think of. In the end it was decided that we would moor lines of landing craft on the other side of Hamilton Bank off Gilkicker Point, the place where some four hundred years earlier Henry VIII had watched his flagship the *Mary Rose* sink.

The weather before the great invasion was cold and windy, and D-Day had to be delayed. Many of the soldiers huddled in landing craft off the point were sick and miserable, enduring very primitive living conditions with hardly a 'head' between them. Orders came through that I was to ferry as many troops as possible to Southsea Common and let them have a run. Suddenly the order was countermanded. It appeared the army commanders feared that once landed there was no way our troops would return to their unstable craft, pitching and tossing in the Channel sea.

After D-Day Portsmouth remained busy, with further waves of troops and equipment being shipped to the Normandy beaches. One evening I had a grim reminder of the battles waged on the other side. An oceangoing tug entered the harbour and moored on a jetty allocated to another ship. I had an urgent message from the harbour master: 'Get the tug moved immediately!'

Commandeering a launch, I went alongside and climbed on

board. There was no one on the tug except for thirty-two corpses lying on the deck. What was I to do with the corpses, never mind the tug? The barracks didn't want to know, neither did the dockyard, and an incredulous funeral director implied that I had gone mad. Finally, Hasler Hospital agreed to take the bodies and provide transport. In the morning the crew drifted back to their ship. I was told that there had been dead men everywhere in the water and that the few found alive had been transferred to an American hospital ship.

When it was apparent that the invasion was going to succeed, the pressure on our band of auxiliary pilots receded and we even had the odd day's leave so I could return to Brighton or Gladys could visit Portsmouth. Better still, we rented a small flat in Portsmouth's old town where Gladys and I could be alone together for the first time since our honeymoon. I was very fond of Albert and Ethel, but we wanted a bit of space and Albert was wont to spend a mighty long time in the bathroom.

The war was going well, but the arrival of the doodlebugs (V1s) from Germany in mid June was a nasty shock. They had a very distinctive engine noise. You were safe enough while you could hear the engine but when it stopped the doodlebug would crash, and doodlebugs carried a large cache of explosive. At night a red flame from the back of each one would light up the sky and leave a trail behind it. Of course it was terrifying, but the British being what they are, many treated it as a spectator sport. 'How many did you see last night?'

The most impressive and formidable operation during those summer months was watching squadron after squadron of Allied heavy bombers flying south to France and beyond. The Lancaster bombers in particular could be heard from miles away, like the approach of an invading army. In a way I suppose that is exactly what they were. We often counted the planes out and the counted them back in. Sometimes it would be obvious that our airmen had paid too heavy a price, and it was not unusual for damaged aircraft to crash on the South Downs as they struggled to gain sufficient height to reach their base.

At the end of 1944 I had a new job as a spare commanding officer for Western Approaches trawlers. In quick succession I commanded HMS *Irwell*, HMS *Cape Mariato*, a ship I had worked with in Canada, HMS *Painter* and HMS *Coldstreamer*. *Coldstreamer* was in a bad state, as for a month the ship had battled with continuous gales in the North Atlantic. Against the odds, the captain had managed to save his ship but at a heavy price – seriously ill and tired out, he had collapsed and been rushed to hospital. The captain had been fortunate that his first lieutenant, who was from the Argentine, was very able and a great character. He had brought a sheep on board in order to give the crew a memorable Christmas dinner. However, by the time Christmas arrived no one had the heart to kill the sheep. Now, so many years later, I rather wished I had asked him how he came to be fighting for the Allies and had ended up on one of our trawlers.

Taking *Coldstreamer* to sea from Plymouth to Liverpool, I asked the chief engineer if all was well.

'If I keep the pumps running she may not sink on this wee voyage, but I'll not vouch for it.'

If anything the ship's condition was worse than the chief had reported, with rivets broken or missing and water pouring in through the hull.

'The trouble is,' said one of the Wallasey dockyard super-intendents when we got there, 'that you have been letting off depth charges too close to the ship.'

'That's bloody nonsense,' I told him, 'and you know it. We would never do such a thing.'

Later the dockyard made amends, and before long I was able to report that HMS *Coldstreamer* was once again ready for war.

The four ships I had captained in the space of ten weeks were very different, but there was humour and fellowship on all the trawlers. Bunches of quirky, tough, brave individuals carried out their orders in the most singular way.

15

My last command

In March 1945 I was appointed commanding officer of HMS *Guardsman,* a real honour as she was cock ship and well known as being one of the most efficient small ships in the Royal Navy. Lieutenant-Commander Linguard, whom I had relieved, had been given the command of a frigate, but on receipt of the news that the king wished to inspect *Guardsman* he was rushed back to Wallasey. I was to lend him his old ship for the day. That was fair enough – he had been a marvellous captain.

That evening there was a reception where all the commanding officers in the port were presented to His Majesty. I thought the king looked much older than when he had given me my medal at Buckingham Palace some four years previously. I remembered that he had served with the British fleet during the great Battle of Jutland when he was a midshipman on the battleship *Collingwood.* Now he was head of state. Never a strong man, he looked strained. The main reason for the king's visit to Liverpool was not to inspect *Guardsman* but to pay tribute to Captain F E Walker, RN, CB, DSO (and three bars) and his men who had done so much to defeat the U-boat menace. Captain Walker's innovation and ideas, especially when he was able to hunt U-boats with two or more ships, had been extraordinarily successful. His ship alone accounted for the destruction of fourteen U-boats; one day he sank one in the morning watch and another in the afternoon. His last job was keeping German U-boats away from the Allied landings in Normandy – not one got through. Walker died in July 1944, aged forty-eight. A driven man, he was worn out and much affected by the loss of his son, Tim, who had been a submariner who had perished when his submarine was lost in the Mediterranean.

I was impressed and proud of my new ship and its weapons, four twin Oerlikons, a 3.7 quick fire, a steam gun and packs of depth charges. Everything worked, and I had a marvellous crew of forty and four officers. Not bad, for someone who had started out as a boy signalman. We all knew that Germany could not hold out for much longer, but there was much speculation as to how many ships, and how many of us, would be expected to sail for the Far East. The war with Japan was still bloody and the outcome uncertain.

In the meanwhile, life on *Guardsman* was little changed and continued much as before. We escorted ships from one port to another and protected them from U-boats as there were still a number of them around our coasts. We also undertook a series of other jobs which Command found for us. One of these was protecting a large cable layer off the coast of Cornwall. There were no incidents, but it was interesting to see how the work was done and to witness the cable layer's pinpoint navigation. I had thought, and I suspect many still do, that the size of a cable being laid across the Atlantic would be substantial – the girth of an elephant's trunk. But no, the cable was little more than a hosepipe and it wasn't laid along the bottom of the seabed but rather draped over the tops of peaks, ridges and undersea mountains while in between it would hang free like a washing line.

There was one run to Liverpool that gave us some excitement. We were escorting a single merchantman northwards when our

```
TO    GUARDSMAN                    FROM:  IRWELL


            Following  received  from C in C W A  begins:
TO   IRWELL (R) FOIC LIVERPOOL              FROM:  C IN C W A

      My  301831 A March Request  you will convey to Commanding Officer
      of HMS GUARDSMAN my congratulations  on the excellent appearance
      of his ship on the occasion of the visition of their Majesties
      the King and Queen  on 27th March DTG 301837 A March  Ends.


                  T.O.O.  302150 A March
                  T.O.R.  011035 A April
```

Asdic crew picked up a strong echo. I had no doubt that it was a submarine but despite dropping patterns of depth charges we had no success in finding our quarry. I called for help from one of the new hunter–killer groups that Captain F E Walker had set up. Very quickly we were joined by a corvette. Between us we laid several more patterns, but again with no success. The corvette was called to another incident but I was sure that the U-boat was still around and determined to get it if I could. For the next twelve hours we maintained our position.

The following morning I heard a sound like the starting of an engine and then nothing. Was it my imagination? Some of my crew thought so, but I was certain that somewhere close, perhaps sitting on the sea bed, a U-boat had outwitted us. On our return to base I made inquiries.

'Yes, we did have an echo about two miles north of you.'

'So it got away. Why didn't you tell me?'

'We had lots of other things to do, sorry.'

I was disappointed, but the moment had passed. The next day we were detailed to escort a Trinity House ship some three hundred miles out at sea where it would report the latest weather conditions and barometric pressures.

At last Victory in Europe Day (VE Day) was declared on 8 May 1945.[11] It had been a long time coming – for the better part of six years we had been at war with Germany. On the following day, VE Day plus one, we were proceeding towards the approaches of Scapa when a German submarine surfaced and approached *Guardsman*, flying a tattered black flag. U-boat U2334 surrendered to us without fuss or bother and obeyed every instruction.

I went on board the submarine to have a look. Living on a trawler was no picnic, but preferable in every way to this small U-boat, which was cramped beyond measure with little room to move and hardly any food, and where most tasks had to be done

---

[11] Following Hitler's suicide, Grand Admiral Dönitz agreed the unconditional surrender of all German forces. It was Dönitz who had controlled the German submarine fleet and led the attack on the American eastern seaboard.

manually. But, small as it was, the U-boat could have been a real threat, its torpedoes capable of wreaking havoc and destruction and sinking the largest of ships. The U-boat's captain told me something about himself. He was in his early twenties and had been at university when he was instructed to join the Kriegsmarine (the German navy). He had been trained in the Baltic and in a relatively short time had been appointed commander of his own submarine, albeit a very small one.

Had he succeeded in any of his torpedo attacks?

'No.'

Had he fired any torpedoes?

'No.'

What were his problems in mounting an attack?

'Mosquitoes. They come at us so quickly, so low and fast, that we hardly hear them. Several times we were hit by their fire' – and he showed me his conning tower, which was riddled with holes.

I felt no anger towards the man, and neither did our crew, despite the terrible things that their country had done to their prisoners, including women and children. When shown pictures of Belsen our German captives were visibly shocked but dismissed them as Allied propaganda. Surely they must have known? But when it came to it they were sailors, men like us, living a hard, rough life. There is a fellowship amongst those who are tested by the sea.

When we arrived at Scapa a boarding party took charge of the U-boat and we were told to proceed directly to St Anne's Harbour, Alderney in the Channel Islands. We were to escort a party of army engineers who were collecting stores and vehicle parts from the occupied island. 'We're particularly after the German trailers, which are the right size and much better than ours,' explained a major in charge.

I was lucky enough to find a small staff car in which I was driven round the island. I was astonished at the fortifications – gun emplacements with 10-foot solid concrete walls and guns such as one might find on a battleship. Todt, the major German building and engineering company, had built the fortifications using slave labour. Many had died from beatings and starvation. Food in the last few months was almost non-existent, not just for the prisoners but also for the guards and the small group of islanders who had elected to remain during the occupation. The guards were now the prisoners, and I wondered what would happen to them.

Out of nowhere I had a sudden, wild thought – why not take the car back to England? All I had to do was to have it lowered onto the foredeck. It would be captain's booty, and why not? Alas, when I got to the harbour the tide had gone out. Its rise and fall can be over forty feet in the Channel Islands, and there was no way the car could be lowered onto the *Guardsman* from that height.

'Will you take it back to England for me?' I asked the major in charge.

'Certainly not!'

After our foray to Alderney we were based at Plymouth for a while before being ordered back to Loch Alsh, where some forty captured U-boats had been collected. Arrangements had been made for these U-boats to be taken from Loch Alsh across to Lough Foyle in Northern Ireland. Units of the British fleet, ourselves, destroyers, an aircraft carrier, corvettes, cruisers and converted fishing vessels, were to accompany the captured U-boats. It was to be a great day. The Pathe Pictorial News was to film the fleet – the surrender shown in the cinemas for all to see. Leaving Loch Alsh all was ready, but as usual in Scottish waters the weather had other plans. A thick, impenetrable fog came down. For hours at a time we didn't see anything of the submarines or the other ships. It was just a few miles before we got to Loch Foyle that the fog lifted – it was almost a surprise to see that the submarines were still there. So the Pathe Pictorial feature of a British fleet escorting the German U-boats to their destruction was never made. A pity – it would have been a fitting end to what is almost certain to be Britain's last great sea battle.

I thought that at the end of the war it might be difficult to keep our crew together, that everyone would be eager to pack up and go home. Well, of course most of us wanted to go home, but we were prepared to wait our turn to be demobbed. In the meanwhile the crew visibly relaxed, happy to perform such duties as they were given in a good spirit. We had our own football team and worked hard at keeping our crew occupied.

One of our jobs was towing concrete barges from Dartmouth to Tower Bridge.

'We're not supposed to be a bloody tug,' said the coxswain, but laughed as he said it. Actually, it was an interesting exercise which we all enjoyed.

We all listened avidly to the BBC news, to find out what was happening in Japan, and also to learn the result of the general election in July. It was a surprise when Winston Churchill and the Tories were roundly defeated. Opinion was divided on *Guardsman* but many in the country and in the army thought it was time for a change. People had not forgotten the hardship and misery of life in the Depression.

'Your old man has had a good run,' said one of our seamen whom I had told in a weak moment that I had voted Tory. 'He ain't done too bad, but time for 'im to go.'

Just a month later came the news of the two atomic bombs dropped in Japan, first at Hiroshima and then at Nagasaki. A whole city wiped out by a single bomb. I remembered Halifax and the great explosion in 1917, that image of the shadow of a man on the wall. And now these new atomic bombs were so many times more powerful. God help us.

But of course we celebrated VJ Day, and that evening all of us in Liverpool let off every rocket we could find. Here is an extract from our ship's paper, the *Guardsman's Gazette*:

In sinister disguise

Here in strange disguise is seen
The 'Old Man', as he might have been,
If to sail he had begun
'Neath the red rayed Rising Sun;
Or if through freak of some tornado,
The 'Guardsman' served some vile Mikado.
Oriental, spruce and neat,

Moustached and spectacled complete –
How inscrutable the face!
If this were indeed the case
Few on board would care to tarry,
Preferring death by hari-kari.
No need for such extremes as these,
The Skipper is not Japanese,
But is, in somewhat humorous way,
Celebrating VJ day.

And the explanation: dressed as a Japanese officer, I surrendered to HMS *Guardsman* with the articles of surrender written on a roll of toilet paper. I was immediately ordered to walk the plank into the dock.

For some time after the celebration *Guardsman* remained in Liverpool, moored in Gladstone Dock alongside a captured U-boat which had been opened to the public. There were queues of people eager to see the inside of one of those hated submarines.

But sometimes the reactions of those who had climbed on board were unexpected.

'Poor buggers,' said a soldier climbing out of the conning tower, 'they must have shit themselves.'

By late summer most of us on *Guardsman* were thinking about what life would be like on Civvy Street and where we might be able to find a job. The government sent regular bulletins with details of jobs and training opportunities. Perhaps I could become a teacher? During my time in the navy I had become used to instructing recruits. There was a short but intensive course at Bognor Regis Teacher Training College. That sounded interesting. I also thought about working for Alan West, the electrical engineers in Brighton. The firm was well known in navy circles, as almost every piece of electrical equipment used in the navy was stamped 'AW'. By the end of the year I was ready to leave. Of course there was much that I would miss, but it was time to go and I knew it.

I still have my Form S450:

10th December 1945

This is to certify Geoffrey Holder-Jones has served as a Temporary Lieutenant RNVR in HMS *Guardsman* under my command, during which period he has conducted himself to my entire satisfaction. A keen, capable and efficient commanding officer.

Captain, HMS *Columbo*

16

Thirty-nine steps

Well, it was rather more – sixty-nine steps, actually. We had to climb four flights of steep stairs to get to our flat in Compton Road, Brighton, but on the bright side Gladys and I were together, in our own home at the very top of a Victorian terraced house close to Seven Dials. It was little more than an attic, with no bathroom, but we were proud of it. We were still living there when our first and much loved daughter Geraldine was born. Quite how Gladys managed I don't know, but life for most people in those days was very difficult, with a shortage of housing of any kind and food rationing more severe than it had been during the war. A rumour that some liver might be for sale would produce long queues outside a butcher.

But I am getting ahead of myself. In the spring of 1946, for the first time since leaving school, I had nothing to do. I was not worried, I had been accepted for a teacher's training course at Bognor Regis College in the autumn and still had some back pay from the navy. But it came as a shock when Gladys's new job as a telegraphist at the post office was terminated. Gladys was disappointed, as she had enjoyed the work. In those days few people had telephones and urgent messages were delivered by telegraph boys who wore round hats on top of their heads. Unfortunately for Gladys her job was a reserved occupation for those returning from the war. Gladys had done more than most, but those were the rules.

I began to count my money and found I was spending more than I thought. My favourite walk in Brighton was along the sea front, and I noticed that there were a team of workers on the Palace Pier.

'Could you do with a spare hand?' I asked the foreman.

'It's a dirty job and you will be working over the water.'

'I'm quite good at that kind of thing,' I told him.

The job was mine. I was given a plank, a piece of rope and a hammer and began chipping rust and peeling paint with the best of them. It was therapeutic and the pay was one shilling and eleven-and-a-half pennies per hour, plus six pennies an hour danger money for working over water, a better rate of pay than I had been getting while I was commanding officer of *Guardsman*.

I never fell into the water, but it was not uncommon. 'That's what you get the extra six pence for,' one of my colleagues was told when we dragged him out of the sea, frightened and shivering from the cold.

After ten weeks on and under the pier I had a bit of luck. I was told of a short-term vacancy at the Portslade Approved School for Boys. I got the job. I didn't know what to expect but found I liked the boys. They were mischievous and they would pinch anything that came their way – taking them shopping once a week on a Saturday afternoon in Portslade was a nightmare. But most of them had a great sense of humour and would look after their mates through thick and thin. To some extent the school was run on service lines: set times for meals, classes and regular assemblies and parades, which gave the staff an opportunity to see who had absconded. I often asked myself what had gone wrong for them and why they were there. What I did know was that many of them, given a bit of training and discipline and shown some kindness, would have made good and brave shipmates.

The summer was soon over, and in September I joined the Bognor Regis Teacher Training College for a thirteen-month course. 'Bugger Bognor,' George V had famously exclaimed on his deathbed, and he had a point. Still, it wasn't that bad. We had the sea and a splendid park nearby. As it happened I saw little of Bognor; ours was an intensive course and most of us lived in the college. Lectures – or were they lessons? – lasted from 8.30 am to 5.00 pm and then, after an early supper, instruction would carry on into the evening. Saturday was a half day but we were expected to be involved in some kind of sport. On winter afternoons I played rugby for the college, and later in the evening I would face a dilemma: would it be another pint of Harvey's or an early bus to Brighton to see Gladys?

I found the work more difficult than I had expected, and at one time I wondered whether I would pass the course – but in the end all was well. Then came the practical side: a secondment to a school in Horsham and to the County Secondary School for Boys in Portslade. It was then that my time in the navy proved to be of real help. I found that controlling a bunch of sailors and a bunch of schoolboys was much the same. At the end of my training at Portslade the headmaster offered me a job. I still have a picture of myself sitting with my first-year form in 1948, thirty-one boys of mixed ability, the same number as my crew in HMS *Baffin*.

Once I had settled into my new role as a teacher, I rejoined the Royal Navy Volunteer Reserve, but this time in Sussex. Our base was the old RNR battery which had been established on Hove seafront since 1905. So there I was back to being a weekend sailor, as my father had called the Reserve some twenty-five years earlier. Of course times had changed, and so had the faces, but I enjoyed the companionship and made new friends. After HMS *Axford*, the Division's tender was a purpose-built minesweeper, HMS *Curzon*, moored in Shoreham Harbour. On a dark and windy night *Curzon* brought back memories – she could roll like a pig, sometimes losing suction when without warning the engines would pack up. Alarming at the best of times, but especially so on a lee shore or in a busy shipping lane.

We in the Sussex Division were very fortunate and enjoyed many visits to friendly ports just across the Channel: Dieppe, Ostend, St Malo, Cherbourg, Bénodet, the Channel Islands. I particularly enjoyed our visits to Ostend, where many of the Belgian officers had served in the Royal Navy during the war. In addition to the weekend training every reservist was obliged to do two weeks full-time in the service. We in Sussex specialised in minesweeping, a vital job still carried out by reservists, more recently after the Gulf Wars in the Gulf of Aqaba.

Much as I enjoyed life in the Sussex Division, my career as a schoolteacher began to take up more and more of my time, and after a few years I had to resign from the RNVR. Also, Gladys and I had another daughter, Judy, a sister for Geraldine. There was nothing for it, we had to move from our lofty attic. Eventually we found a house in Foredown Road, Portslade, which was a good deal cheaper than anything we had looked at in Brighton.

MINISTRY OF DEFENCE (NAVY DEPARTMENT)
WHITEHALL, LONDON, S.W.1.

N/N2/ACR 10151/65/A   6th January 1966

Sir,

    I am commanded by the Admiralty Board of the Defence Council to convey their formal approval to your being placed on the Retired List of the Royal Naval Reserve with effect from 11th December 1965, at your own request, in the rank of Lieutenant Commander.

2.   The Admiralty Board desire me to express their appreciation of your services on the Active List of the Royal Naval Reserve. I am to add that, provided you will report to the Admiral Commanding Reserves annually (between 1st January and 31st March) your name will be retained in the Navy List.

    I am, Sir,
    Your obedient Servant,

Iansarconala

Lieutenant Commander G.H. Jones, DSM, VRD, RNR
103 Foredown Drive
Portslade
Brighton
Sussex

But before I left the RNVR I was witness to two memorable events. First, the coronation of Her Majesty Queen Elizabeth II on 2 June 1953, an appalling day when it rained and rained. Our sailors of course looked immaculate – that was until on closer inspection one saw the white blanco from their hats running down their faces. There were many contingents from abroad, friendly faces from India, Pakistan, Australia, Canada, New Zealand, Africa and all over the world. By then, sadly, a number of countries had already left the British Empire, but for all that it was a grand show. The Queen of Tonga took the biscuit by waving to the crowds with the hood of her carriage wound down so she could be seen by everyone. Just a year later, on Horse Guards Parade, I attended the Jubilee Review of the Royal Naval Volunteer Reserve by Her Majesty the Queen. Before the parade we had a day, or was it two days, being drilled at Portsmouth Naval Barracks. Drill had never been a speciality of the RNVR, although the Royal Marine Reserves were excellent.

I found my last dinner as an active member at the Reserve emotional, and thought that it would be the last occasion I would ever sing 'Sussex by the sea' together with my colleagues. But no, here I am another thirty years on, and together with Gladys I attend the reunion dinners whenever I can. I am nearly blind and very deaf, but I can still follow the song:

Far o'er the seas we wander,
Wide through the world we roam,
Far from the kind hearts yonder,
Far from the dear old home.

On retirement, I had a polite letter from the Admiralty thanking me for my services. That's that, I thought, I'll close the file. But the Admiralty didn't close theirs. In 2005 I received a large medal from the Russian Federation in commemoration of the sixtieth anniversary of the victory of the Great Patriotic War, 1941–1945.

Good of them to remember me, I thought.

The Admiralty, however, were somewhat dubious and issued a directive: 'We must make it clear that this commemorative medal is not to be worn with your British decorations.'

Actually it's rather an ugly medal and it doesn't go with those

I've got. But what the hell, I've got half a mind to wear it should a suitable occasion arise.

There were not many days when I didn't recall my time at sea, but my time as a schoolmaster became just as important to me. I like to think that the children I taught enjoyed the times we had together.

My second teaching job was as an assistant at St Nicholas Church of England Primary School. Here again there was a good staff and a good atmosphere. I could quite happily have stayed there, but then came an approach from the head of St Andrew's Church of England School in Hove. Would I like to apply for the headmaster's vacancy? This gave rise to a ditty which became well-known in our small circle:

> Said St Andrew to St Nicholas, 'I really need a head.'
> 'What about young Holder-Jones? I wonder if instead
> Of teaching at your place he'd take command of mine?'
> Said St Nicholas to Andrew, 'That's a selfish thought of thine,
> The gain would all be on your side, and none at all on mine.'

And so in 1958 I became, and for the next twenty-two years remained, the headmaster of St Andrew's School. During my time there the school building was knocked down and rebuilt. Inevitably this entailed consultations and arguments with councillors, planners, builders and architects, bureaucracy enough to drive one mad, and of course it meant I spent less time teaching.

And so life went on. Gladys and I worked as volunteers at Worthing Hospital for some twenty-five years. We were even given a certificate of long service, which is pasted in my scrapbook. It wasn't a trial, it wasn't a chore, and we met many wonderful doctors and nurses and brave patients who met their fate with a smile and a nod. And sometimes patients so ill it seemed certain they must die, recovered and walked out of hospital on their own two feet. Those were special moments. I've got a lot to be thankful for. Old age, the bugger, has of course taken its toll and gradually I've lost most of my vision. But St Dunstan's, the hospital for blind ex-serviceman, has been wonderful. Perhaps most importantly, they have given me the confidence to carry on and not give up.

Through all these years Gladys has been by my side, helping me in so many ways. I am very proud of her and my two daughters, Geraldine and Judy, who give us joy.

So what now? Gladys and I are booked to join a cruise on one of those liners which zigzag across the world from one port to another. Our sea time, we call it, and this time it is to be the eastern Mediterranean. The crew will be extraordinarily kind – nothing is too much trouble – but the thing Gladys I will really appreciate is the warmth. Last winter was damn cold and we felt it.

And that is the story of Lieutenant-Commander Geoffrey Holder-Jones, once a boy signalman. My adventures are perhaps best encapsulated in two poems. The second is the poem I've already shared with you, penned by my old friend Michael Thwaites who for some two years was first lieutenant on *Wastwater*, but the first is that wonderful poem by John Masefield in which you can hear the sea breaking over the bows of the little British coaster as she battles through the waves.

Extract from **Cargoes**, *by John Masefield*

Dirty British coaster with a salt-caked smoke stack,
Butting through the Channel in the mad March days,
With a cargo of Tyne coal,
Road-rail, pig-lead,
Firewood, iron-ware, and cheap tin trays.

Coming into the Clyde, *by Michael Thwaites*

Part of me for ever is the January morning
Coming into the Clyde in the frosty moonlight
And the land under snow and the snow under moonlight,
Fall upon fall, a soundless ecstasy.
I alone on the bridge, below me the helmsman
Whistling softly to the listening voice pipe,
And no sound else than the washing of the bow-wave
As the buoys go by like marching pylons.
I gaze from the glory of the bared universe
To the guarded secret of the winter world
Rapt, and the helmsman now is silent,
And I wait for the time to alter course.
To port left the magic scenario mountains
White above the shoulders of holy island,
And nearer, clear as a square-lined coverlet,
All the fields and hedges on the slopes of Arran.
But further and smaller, away to starboard
The plaited hills of Ayrshire gleam,
And I in thought am over them all
Away to my darling and my little son.
Beyond the moonlit hills that morning
My darling lay, and my little son;
But she in her cold bed lone and waking,
And he in the frozen ground asleep.

Tim Parker

Tim Parker was born in 1933, and his early memories include living in Stockport, near Manchester, where his mother's family firm made hats. For his twenty-first birthday he was given a bowler hat with extra rabbit fur 'for best'. Among his many aunts and uncles was Cecil Parker, who had broken his neck in the First World War trenches but went on to become a leading and well-loved actor in the 1940s and 50s.

While at Harrow School Tim joined the RNVR in London's HMS *President*, and two years later he was promoted to Midshipman RNVR. After National Service a variety of jobs included working for ICI and the Rank Organisation. In the early 1960s he moved to Brighton, where he has lived ever since. In 1970 he and his wife Beth planted a vineyard, one of the first in the country. He would like every reader of this book to drink English wine!

At the age of 67, Tim started writing the regular 'Parker's Progress' column for the Brighton *Argus*. This is his first book.

DRINK UP AND BE A MAN
Memoirs of a steward and
engine-room hand

JOHN J MAHON

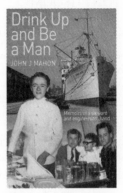

Born into poverty in Ireland in the 1940s, John J Mahon
stands only four feet nine and a half inches tall. He went
to sea as a steward on passenger liners at the age of 17, and
later served on a variety of ships as a donkeyman, greaser
and engine-room hand. During a 20-year seagoing career,
he overcame his sense of inferiority but not the lure of
alcohol – until he came ashore. The true story of one man's triumph against the
odds, a vivid portrayal of life in Ireland, in London, and at sea.

> **'John Mahon was one of those seafarers who left a great
> impression upon my life'**
> – Terry Simco, OBE

Illustrated · UK ISBN 978-1-906266-19-6 pbk

PIRACY TODAY
Fighting villainy
on the high seas

JOHN C PAYNE

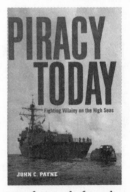

In recent years, piracy at sea has become as much of a
peril as terrorism. Modern piracy is far removed from the
romance of the pirate in popular culture. It is a billion-
dollar business that takes advantage of inadequate
international law, lax enforcement and under-crewed
ships. Heavily armed gangs have been emboldened by
successes in being paid off with six-figure ransoms. As the cost of cargo thefts and
insurance premiums rises, so does the physical danger to mariners worldwide. This
eye-opening account, which details hundreds of recent incidents, brings decades of
experience to bear on looking at what is being done – and what more can be done.

> **'A comprehensive survey ... *Piracy Today* will help
> travelers and businessmen chart a safe course'**
> – *Wall Street Journal*

> **'Timely, authoritative, well-written and downright scary ...'**
> – Ian Scott, former Director of the World Bank

Illustrated · US / UK ISBN 978-1-57409-291-2 hbk

DIVER

TONY GROOM

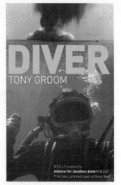

An honest, moving and sometimes hilarious account of a hair-raisingly exciting career, both in the Royal Navy and in commercial deep-sea diving – training the most unlikely of raw recruits ... handling unexploded bombs while under air attack in the Falklands... living for months in a pressurised bottle with a voice like Donald Duck ... commuting to work through a hole in the floor in the freezing, black depths of the North Sea. Tony Groom joined the Royal Navy at the age of seventeen and became a member of the Fleet Clearance Diving Team. After leaving the Navy in 1985, he travelled the world as a commercial diver.

> **'The Royal Navy Clearance Divers, not the SAS, are the British mystery unit of the Falklands War'**
> – Major General Julian Thompson

> **'Wide-ranging, illuminating and sympathetic ... this tale fills a massive gap and is long overdue'**
> – Commodore Michael C Clapp

With a foreword by ADMIRAL SIR JONATHON BAND

Illustrated · UK ISBN 978-1-906266-06-6 pbk · US ISBN 978-1-57409-269-1 pbk

JOSEPH CONRAD: MASTER MARINER

PETER VILLIERS

Before he published his first novel in 1895, Joseph Conrad spent 20 years in the merchant navy, eventually obtaining his master's ticket and commanding the barque *Otago*. This book, superbly illustrated with paintings by Mark Myers, traces his sea-career and shows how Konrad Korzeniowski, master mariner, became Joseph Conrad, master novelist. Alan Villiers, world-renowned author and master mariner under sail, was uniquely qualified to comment on Conrad's life at sea, and the study he began has been completed by his son, Peter Villiers.

> **'A book that finally does justice to Conrad's time at sea'**
> *Traditional Boats and Tall Ships*

Illustrated with 12 paintings in full colour by Mark Myers RSMA F/ASMA
Illustrated · UK ISBN 0-9547062-9-3 pbk · US ISBN 1-57409-244-8 pbk

ICE BEARS AND KOTICK

PETER WEBB

This is the story of an impossible boat journey that two men made for the fun of it. They rowed and sailed through pack ice, and survived polar bears, whales, starvation and capsize – and in so doing they completed the first circumnavigation of the Arctic island of Spitsbergen in an open row boat. Along the way they learned about themselves, about life, and experienced a wilderness that will most likely disappear before the century is out. A story for small-boat sailors, lovers of ice and snow, and anybody who knows anybody who wanted to run away to sea.

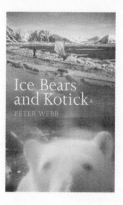

Illustrated • UK ISBN 978-1-906266-03-5 pbk • USA ISBN 978-1-57409-264-6 pbk

THE UNLIKELY VOYAGE OF JACK DE CROW
A Mirror odyssey from north Wales to the Black Sea

A J MACKINNON

A couple of quiet weeks on the River Severn was the intention. 'Somehow things got out of hand,' writes A J Mackinnon. 'A year later I had reached Romania was still going. Equipped with his cheerful optimism and a pith helmet, this Odysseus in a Mirror dinghy takes you with him – 4,900 kilometres over salt and fresh water, through numerous trials and adventures. An epic voyage, brilliantly told.

> **'This is a wonderful idea for a book – a series of ever bolder improvisations in the face of adversity, undertaken in praise of the spirit of adventure'**
> – *Times Literary Supplement*

> **'He must be considered the Captain Slocum of the inland waterways of Europe. If you want a good read, go and buy this book'**
> – *Royal Naval Sailing Association Journal*

Illustrated with maps and line drawings by the author
UK ISBN 0-95381-805-5 pbk • US ISBN 1-57409-152-2 pbk